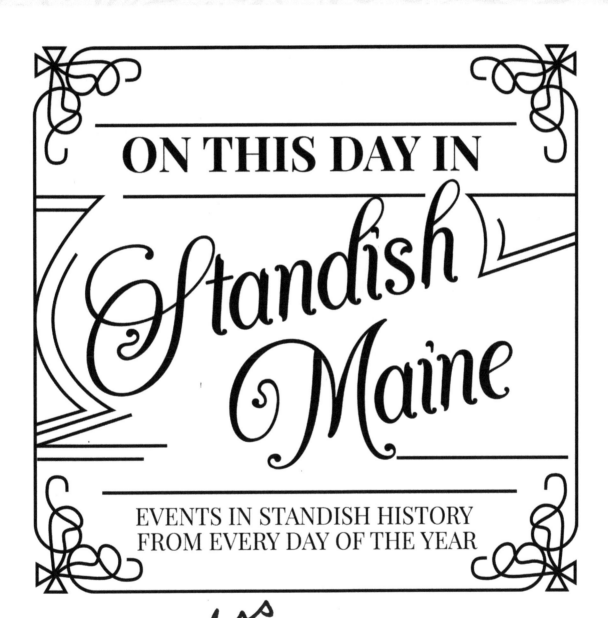

ON THIS DAY IN

Standish Maine

EVENTS IN STANDISH HISTORY FROM EVERY DAY OF THE YEAR

By Bruce L. Douglass
Standish Historical Society

Edited by Lil Barcaski

Published by: GWN Publishing
www.GWNPublishing.com

Cover Design: Kristina Conatser

ISBN: 978-1-959608-91-2 - paperback
ISBN: 978-1-959608-92-9 - hard cover

DEDICATION

This book is dedicated to my wife Cynthia Douglass who encourages me, the members of the Standish Historical Society who keep Standish History alive, and my many former students and former student-athletes from whom I continually draw inspiration.

Table of Contents

Introduction

Something happens somewhere, every single day. From the mundane to the momentous, it doesn't matter, as almost everything is lost or forgotten with the passage of time. Every one of those daily events were notable in someone's life and sometimes of interest to the rest of us. Thankfully, we have diaries, scrapbooks, newspaper clippings, town records, photos, books, and other items that have kept the record of those events. Some of those events just happen to be interesting and offer a glimpse of a town's history and its people. For example, Standish, Maine began as Pearsontown, a reward from the State of Massachusetts to Captains Moses Pearson and Humphrey Hobbs and their men for their actions at the Siege of Louisbourg, Cape Breton Island in1745. Pearsontown became Standish, in honor of Miles Standish, upon incorporation in 1785. In the 250 years or so since then, something interesting happened in Standish on every day of the year!

The Standish Historical Society has a mission to preserve and present the history of Standish, Maine. This honor has been entrusted to us by the town of Standish and the present and former members of the Standish community. We hold thousands of photos of Standish and its people as well as tens of thousands of pieces of paper, from payment orders and receipts to newspaper clippings and more. Our active volunteers staff the Old Red Church Museum in Standish. The Old Red Church was built in 1805 as the first Parish Church of Standish. It housed Standish Academy from 1847 to 1857 on its second floor and Standish High School from 1893 to 1916. It has changed little since those days and is very much worth a visit.

Who am I? I am, admittedly, more than a bit attention deficit, a graduate of Scarborough High School where I played trumpet in the band and ran track and Cross Country. I then attended The University of Maine where I majored in Chemistry Education and again ran track and cross country, and also studied Marine Science at Eastern Connecticut State University. My postgraduate work at the University of Connecticut was in Sport Biomechanics and Exercise Physiology. I am a former high school chemistry teacher and girls' cross country and track coach teaching at Ledyard High School in Ledyard, Connecticut for 44 years. I earned National Coach of the Year honors while I continued to train and compete nationally in Racewalking until transitioning to administration for USA Track & Field as the National Chairman of Racewalking and later as the International Competition Committee Chairman. I am a lifelong genealogist, and avid reader. Now I'm retired and I get to spend my time working with the Standish Historical Society!

This book is just a day to day, every day of the year, sampling of events that have happened in Standish. I call it a "non-calendar." We are including many interesting events, mostly long since forgotten, that should be shared. All the money raised from the sales of this book goes to the Standish Historical Society to maintain our historical collection and museum as well as for our building fund. Since the Old Red Church has no heat or air conditioning, running water, or bathroom facilities, we need to find or build a building to properly store our massive collection and also free up space in the museum.

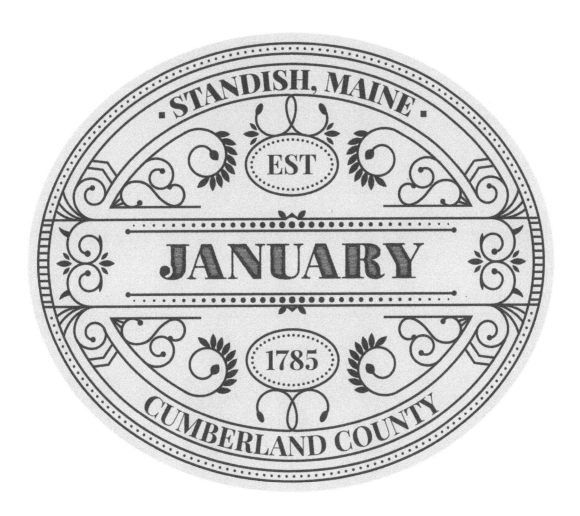

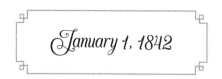

January 1, 1842

William Sanborn, a bounty for Silk.

I hereby certify that I have raised within this state, eight and one fourth pounds of Cocoons for which I claim the bounty allowed by Law of the Town Treasurer of Standish. I also certify that I have reeled from cocoons raised in this State, nine and one half ounces of Silk - **William Sanborn**

Cumberla s Js   January 1st 1842, then personally appeared the above named William Sanborn and made oath that the above certificates are true - Before me, **Phineas Ingalls**, Justice of the Peace

Rec'd of P. Ingalls, Treasurer Sixty Five cents for the bounty within claimed - by me William Sanborn

In 1836, Maine offered a silk bounty of 5 cents per pound of cocoons and 50 cents per pound of reeled silk. When the bounties were lifted and the industry began to rely heavily on foreign silk, silk production in Maine dwindled. It took about 10,000 cocoons to make one-pound weight of reeled silk.

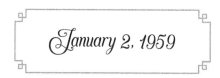

January 2, 1959

School Administrative District No. 6 was formally organized. The district is made of Buxton, Hollis, Standish, Limington and Frye Island. The district schools include: Bonny Eagle High School, Bonny Eagle Middle School, Buxton Center Elementary School, Edna Libby Elementary School, George E. Jack School, H B Emery Junior Memorial School, Hollis Elementary School and Steep Falls Elementary School. It is the largest school district in Maine with approximately 3,500 students.

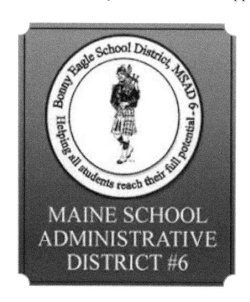

MAINE SCHOOL ADMINISTRATIVE DISTRICT #6

FROM THE DIARIES OF JOHN P. MOULTON

Warm and Pleasant - it thawed in the road. I worked on getting out rollers in the afternoon. Was up to widow Shaw's to a goose party.

The goose party was probably a Mother Goose Party, otherwise known as Old Maid, a card game that first appeared in America, with rules, in 1831. It is speculated that the popular card game might have evolved from a European drinking game.

Ho for Sebago Lake !

GRAND BALL,

MONDAY EVE'G, Jan. 8, '72.

ANNIVERSARY OF

Jackson's Victory at New Orleans,

JANUARY 8, 1815.

Tickets for the Dance $1 00.

MUSIC BY

Manchester's Full Quadrille Band.

Refreshments furnished by Webster, of Fluent Hall An extra train over the P. & O. R. R., will leave P. & K. Depot at 6 45, p. m., stopping at Cumberland Mills, S. Windham and White Rock, for the accommodation of parties wishing to attend the Ball; Returning after the dance. Tickets half fare.
Per Order Committee of Arrangement.
Standish, Jan. 3d, 1872.   ja4td

Portland Daily Press

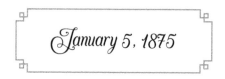

January 5, 1875

Town of Standish to Portland Publishing Company, Publishers of the Portland Daily Press and Maine State Press - To advertise: Child for Adoption

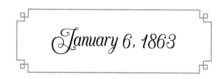

January 6, 1863

FROM THE DIARIES OF JOHN P. MOULTON

Warm but overcast in the afternoon Levi & I commenced making hoops. In the evening was out to Spelling school at the Rich neighborhood schoolhouse.

"Spelling school" could have been in the form of a spelling bee for adults, which became popular in the 1800's, *but it was also likely that it was adult education. From his diaries, which began in the early 1850's, he had few issues with spelling or writing but here he is traveling two to three miles to the Richville schoolhouse (and home) after dark to attend this "school."*

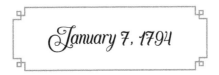

January 7, 1794

To **Peter Moulton** and **Ebenezer Shaw** disinterested and judicious persons both of Standish in the County of Cumberland, greetings: You are hereby appointed and impowered to appraise upon Oath at the true value thereof in Money according to your best judgment, a Stary Steer, one year old last spring, taken up by Sargent Shaw of said Standish, who has entered, posted and cried the same as the law directs - and you are to make return of this warrant and your doings, thereon into the Town Clerk's Office of said Standish, within seven days from the date hereof.... ....Pursuant to the within warrant we have appraised the beast within mentioned at £ 1-14, fees 4/ , Peter Moulton & Ebenezer Shaw.

In 1794 the British currency system was still being used. The appraisal was 1 pound 14 shillings and the fees were, 4/, 4 shillings no pence. There were 20 shillings to the pound and 12 pennies to the shilling.

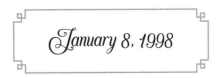

January 8, 1998

Standish (and the whole of Maine) got hit with a massive ice storm. Over three days of snow and freezing rain, felled trees and, of course, power lines, leaving many in the dark for as long as two weeks.

To the Honorable Senate and House of Representatives of the State of Maine in Legislature assembled. Humbly represent **Jonathan Moore, Josiah Paine, Thomas Leavitt, Enoch Boothby, Theopolis Waterhouse, William Spear, Silas Berry, Benjamin McCorrison, Joseph McCorrison** and **Peter Paine**, inhabitants of the town of Buxton in the county of York, that owing to their peculiar situation, they are subjected to heavy and numerous grievances, of which from your honors they respectfully pray redress by dividing them from the said town of Buxton, and annexing them to the town of Standish in the County of Cumberland, agreeable to the bounds hereon after named, ..." Passed by the Senate, January 8th, and by the House January 9th.

(The basic grievances were the distances they were required to travel for court, town meetings, militia training, musters, and schools.)

**Standish High School
1918**

January 10, 1882

Notice of Foreclosure.

WHEREAS, SARAH A. RAND, of Standish, in the County of Cumberland and State of Maine, by her deed, dated June 6th, 1872, recorded in Cumberland Registry of Deeds, Book 391, Page 358, conveyed to me the undersigned, in mortgage, a certain parcel of real estate, situated in Standish, in the County of Cumberland: the same being the one-hundred acre lot of land, numbered one hundred and ten in the third division of lots in said Standish, with all the building on the same, and is the same premises conveyed to John C Dyer, by Theophilus Dyer and Abigail Dyer, by deed dated May 12th, 1868, and recorded in the Cumberland Registry of Deeds, Book 368, Page 428. The condition of said mortage having been broken, I the undersigned, by reason thereof, claim a foreclosure.

LEMUEL RICH, 3d.

Standish January 3d, 1882. jan4dlaw3wW*

Portland Daily Press

January 11, 1950

A Quit Claim deed was signed by the Society for the Preservation of New England Antiquities (SPNEA) to the Town of Standish for the Land for the George E. Jack School. The land was given to SPNEA in the will of **Frances S. Marrett** (which included the Marrett house). The Conveyance was made for a school, park, playground or municipal purposes and reverts to SPNEA if it is not used for such for a period of five years.

Daniel Marrett House

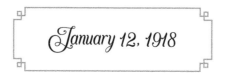

January 12, 1918

The Town of Standish received a bill from Attorney **Frank M. Haskell**, for among other things: On April 30, 1916 for a letter of advice and services drafting a permit to carrying fire arms; and May 10, 1916, consultation and advice regarding electric lighting rights of way.

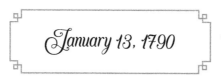

January 13, 1790

Sir, please to pay to Sargent Shaw sixteen shillings and six pence for finding glass for the schoolhouse. - To Mr. **Theodore Mussey**, Town Treasurer. **Thomas Shaw** & **Peter Moulton**, selectmen.

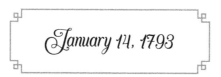

January 14, 1793

Cumberland County ss. To the Constable of the Town of Standish: Greetings,

You are directed in the name of the Commonwealth of Massachusetts to warn and give notice unto **Nathaniel Rand** of Gorham in the County of Cumberland Laborer who has lately come into this town for the purpose of abiding therein not having obtained the towns consent therefor that he depart the limits there within fifteen days.

And of this precept, with your doings thereon, you are to make return into the office of the Clerk of the town within twenty days next coming that such further proceedings may be had in the premises as the law directs given under our hand and Seal at Standish aforesaid this 14th Day of January AD 1793,

Selectmen of   Peter Moulton

said Town   Geo Freeman

Cumberland ss. Standish Jany. 14, 1793.

In obedience to the within, I have warned the within named Nathaniel Rand to depart this town

Simeon Sanborn, Constable

> **Nathaniel Rand** *was born in Gorham in 1774 and married* **Dorcas Hamblen** *in Gorham in 1798. He was living in Standish by the 1810 Census and*

Oak Hill Road 1870's

**Cobb-Buzzell House and orchard (center)
Blacksmith shop on the corner of Rt 25 and Oak Hill Rd**

died there in 1825. He is buried in the Rand Family Cemetery in Standish. He served in the War of 1812 in Captain John York's Company, Lt. Colonel J. *Burbank's Regiment. His family line in Standish is extensive.*

January 15, 1990

The Sebago Lake Church Fire. Miraculously, an 19th century bible survived the fire - untouched by flame or water. It is currently displayed at the Old Red Church.

January 16, 1855

FROM THE DIARIES OF JOHN P. MOULTON OF SEBAGO LAKE VILLAGE

"Fell off Alinda. In the evening went to writing school. It snowed in the evening. That evening felt a shock of an earthquake.

(Alinda was probably a horse, writing school was probably like adult education).

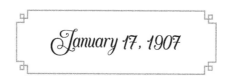

FROM THE DIARY OF GILBERT MOULTON OF SEBAGO LAKE VILLAGE

The coldest day for the winter - was on the route until 3-20PM around home rest of day and evening. The thermometer was 12 below zero here, 28 below at **Laura Sanborn**'s, 22 below at **Almon Marean**'s, 28 below at **Frank Pendexter**'s, 30 below at **Chadbourne**'s, 58 below at Beacher Falls VT. It is a little warmer tonight. It has not got down to zero at 9 pm.

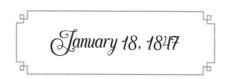

FROM GARDNER DENNETT'S ACCOUNT LEDGER

Seth Higgins purchased a bottle of Down's Elixir for 50¢ and **Reuben Lowell** purchased 2 quarts of gin @40¢, 2 quarts of Rum @45¢ and 2 quarts of Whiskey @45¢.

Rev. **N. H. Down**'s *Elixir was touted as a sure cure for coughs, colds, Whooping cough and all lung diseases including consumption or Tuberculosis. It contained 11 1/2% alcohol with one grain of opium. Reuben Lowell ran a nearby inn so his purchase was for sale to his patrons.*

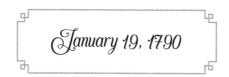

To Mr. Theodore Mussey Town Treasurer, Sir, please to pay Thomas Shaw five shillings, six pence that being due him for making one thousand shingles for the schoolhouse on the northeast rode. Peter Moulton & Josiah Shaw, Selectmen.

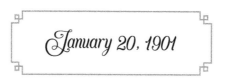

FROM THE DIARY OF GILBERT MOULTON OF SEBAGO LAKE VILLAGE

Clowdy and very cold. It was 18 below zero here this morning, at home, all day and evening. It is a little warmer. Tonight it was 25 below zero.

The Richville Chapel was dedicated with the Rev. **C. E. Harmon** of North Scarborough, Rev. **Staples** of East Raymond, Rev. **A. E. Cox** of Steep Falls, Rev. **Ozro Roys** of Livermore Falls, Rev. **Cogswell** of Standish and Rev. **Samuel B. Sawyer** in attendance. In 1895, horse sheds were built to shelter the animals from the elements.

Richville

FROM THE AUTOGRAPH BOOK OF NELLIE A. SHAW

May your joys be as deep as the ocean, and your sorrows as light as its foam. Is the wish of your friend. **George W. Legrow**, Standish;

Love God and keep his command, Nellie. It's the wish of your friend, **Jane N. Blake** 73 years old.

Nellie Ada Shaw *was born in Westbrook August 9, 1872, the daughter of* **Samuel and Hester Berry Shaw**. *She married* **Herbert L. Rich**, *son of* **Granville and Abby Hamlin Rich**, *on October 21, 1900 in Standish and died May 24, 1965 in Standish at the age of 92. She is buried in Hamlin Cemetery.* **George W. LeGrow** *was a Portland native, born there in 1874. He would have been 11 years-old when he signed the book.* **Jane Newbegin Blake** *was born April 17, 1812, the daughter of* **John and Rhuhannah Whitmer Newbegin**. *In 1838, she married* **Reuben Blake** *in Windham. She died November 22, 1893 at 81 years. George W. LeGrow was Jane Blake's grandson through her daughter* **Delphinia** *who married* **Benjamin LeGrow**.

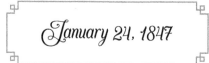

January 23, 1906

Ginn and Company, publisher of school and college textbooks received payment for book purchases by **E. P. Goodwin**, principal of Standish High. Looking at this long list from this one publisher can give an indication of what was taught at Standish High School. Keeping in mind that there were only two teachers, Principal E. P. Goodwin and Teacher **Mona Hartford** of the 25-30 students in grades 9-12, the subjects included English History, American History, Geography, Spelling, Arithmetic, Plane Geometry, Inorganic Chemistry & Lab, German and Latin. We know that also taught were Physiology, Botany, Physics, Literature and more.

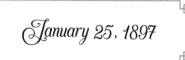

January 24, 1847

Certain residents of the Steep Falls community with elder **Andrew Hobson** as moderator and Elder **Peltiah Hobson** as clerk met at the "Old Red Hall" to determine the expediency of organizing a church. The Red Hall was owned by **Jebez Hobson** and during the early period of religious worship in the community the second floor of this building was frequently used as the meeting place of the followers of the Freewill Baptist faith. This hall was located between the Limington end of the covered bridge, which then spanned the Saco River and the house now (1937) owned and occupied by Mr. and Mrs. **C. A. Nason**.

January 25, 1897

Albion Parrish Howe died in Cambridge MA at age 79.

Albion Parrish Howe had a storied military career starting with the War with Mexico in 1847 at age 29, In 1855, he was a part of the Expedition against the Sioux Indians in the Battle of Blue Water. He was at Harper's Ferry, John Brown's raid, in October 1858, and during the Civil was he fought at the Siege of Yorktown, the Battles of Williamsburg, Manassas, South Mountain, Antietam, Fredericksburg, Marye's Heights, Salem, and Gettysburg, having been promoted to Brigadier General and then Major General and Commander of the 2nd Sixth Corps, Army of the Potomac. With the assassination of President Lincoln, he was called to Washington to

take part in the investigation and he was one of the twelve soldiers in the Guard of Honor who escorted the remains of the President from Washington to Springfield, as well as a member of the Court which tried the Lincoln Conspirators.

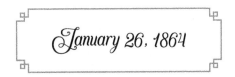

January 26, 1864

EXCERPT FROM A LETTER FROM WILLIAM MANCHESTER JR. TO HIS PARENTS AND BROTHERS FROM CAMP NEAR MITCHELL STATION, VA.

"...The health of the regiment is good. It numbers about 2100, our company 37 men. Jell was in here last night and we made pudding and had some hearty laughs. We made it of bread and apples. We bake beans four times a week and have them as nice as you ever saw. We are living well and expect to be paid off next month. The rebs are coming in as fast as they can get in and my courage is good..."

William Manchester Jr. *enlisted as a private in Co. F 16th ME Infantry on August 14, 1862 at the age of 23. He was promoted to full corporal in 1863. He was wounded on May, 8, 1864 at Laurel Hill VA, the wound was a gunshot to the right hand.*

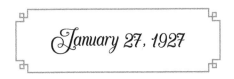

January 27, 1927

"Thermometers registered 30 below here (Steep Falls) this morning."

Portland Evening Express

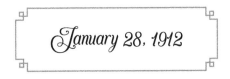

January 28, 1912

STANDISH MAN SHOT BY AN ALLEGED YEGG

Battle in the Woods Near Sebago Lake

Gang of Five Overpowered -- Taken To Village

Wounded Man's Lung Penetrated But He May Recover

Alexander Rosborough, driver of a logging team, lies at the home of **Marshall R. Higgins** near Sebago Lake with a bullet wound in his right lung received late yesterday afternoon while helping run down five yeggmen who are suspected of having robbed the post office and two stores at West Buxton. The desperadoes, who were pursued for four miles in the woods between the Chadbourne neighborhood in Standish and the village of North Windham, were finally cornered by four citizens of Sebago lake and surrendered, being brought to the county jail last night by Sheriff **Lewis W. Moulton** and Deputy Sheriff **Eugene Harmon**.

Rosborough was shot by a man giving his name as **Fred R. Dixon** of Canada, Dixon and **John T. Ryan**, who claims to belong in Berlin N.H., being the only members of the gang who were armed. Dixon fired three times with a double action revolver, the first shot apparently being intended for **Asa Douglass** a clerk in the Sebago Lake Post Office and the General Store conducted by Postmaster **Lemuel Rich**. When Rosborough, whose only weapon was a "peavy" or lumberman's cant dog, which he took from his team, tried to head off the quintet of yeggs, Dixon fired at him twice, one bullet going through his coat and the other hitting him in the right breast.

The wounded man was taken to the Doctor **William S. Thompson** of Standish was called. He probed for the bullet for some time but was unable to find it, and last night he and Dr. **Leonard O. Buzzell** of

Lemuel Rich

Standish and Dr. **Parker** of Windham worked over Rosborough locating the bullet in the vicinity of the shoulder blade.

NOT CRITICAL

While Rosborough's condition is not considered critical, it is serious enough to warrant taking him to a hospital and he will be brought to this city sometime today. The physicians said last night that they believed he will recover unless he took cold and pneumonia developed. In that case, his chance of getting well would be rather slim.

The capture of the five men was one of the most sensational occurrences in Standish in a good many years, and on all sides, the four boys who rounded them up are being complimented for the pluck that they showed in setting out after them and sticking right to the chase until they had got them. Lemuel Rich, the Postmaster, Asa Douglass, his clerk, **Harry Paine**, and **Walter Libby**, a rural mail carrier from the Sebago Lake office, were the men who took their lives in their hands and affected the capture of the alleged burglars, and although they knew that they were in all probability going up against a gang of desperate men who wouldn't hesitate to use gun play if they got within

Dr. Leonard O. Buzzell

range, they didn't falter for an instant after hearing where the suspects were staying.

HAVE BEEN WATCHING

Ever since the robberies at West Buxton, suspicious characters have been seen in the vicinity of Sebago Lake and Standish villages and the people have been on the lookout. Tuesday, **George Thompson** of Standish, son of **Granville Thompson**, was driving in the direction of Sebago Lake when he gave some strangers who are supposed to have been a part of the quintet a ride. At that time, they had a grip but this seems to have disappeared, although, Deputy Sheriff Harmon, before leaving Sebago Lake last night directed that a search be instituted for it. It is possible that the money taken from the West Buxton post office may be in the grip, for the yeggs had very little about them when they were searched at the jail.

SANBORN MET MEN

Albert Sanborn of Sebago Lake also met the men for whom everybody was watching but when he saw them they didn't have any grip. It was generally believed that they were hanging around the community waiting for an opportunity to make a break at either the post office at Sebago Lake or that at Standish village but their hiding place could not be located. Yesterday afternoon, however, a brother of Rosborough, the man who was shot, furnished the first clue to their whereabouts. He saw tracks leading through the snow to the summer camp of **R. H. Soule** of South Windham, which is located near the shore of the lake and instantly reached the conclusion that the men were staying there. He at once notified Libby the mail carrier, who in turn brought the matter to the attention of Postmaster Rich.

CITIZENS ARMED

Within a very short time Rich, Douglass, Libby, and Paine had armed themselves, Libby taking a Winchester rifle and the others Revolvers, and taking a couple of teams, they started for the camp. When they had driven within a short distance of the place, the yeggmen saw them coming and opening the door of their camp they beat a hasty retreat taking to a logging road that ran through the woods. The little posse of citizens urged their horses to a faster pace and the men ahead of them quickened their steps, but they didn't travel so fast as would have expected under the circumstances, apparently being tired.

FOUR MILE CHASE

They managed, though, to give their pursuers a drive of four miles before they were overtaken. Rosborough was coming along the logging road as the man hunt was in progress and he jumped from his team and taking his peavy joined Postmaster Rich's crew. After a while, the yeggs suddenly left the road and started into the woods, and then the other people were obliged to abandon their teams in order to keep up the pursuit. The chase continued for more than a quarter of a mile into the forest before the capture was made.

DIXON PULLED HIS GUN

Dixon pulled his gun when he and his companions saw that the other men were gaining on them and the first shot is believed to have been meant for Douglass. It went wide of the mark. Rosborough, the teamster, in his effort to head off the gang, flourished his peavy and in less time that it takes to tell it, he got his, the first bullet passing through his coat and the second striking him in the breast. Dixon afterwards said he didn't intend to shoot Rosborough but that his gun went off accidentally. The fact that he had previously fired one, though, and that he pulled the trigger twice the next time would not seem to substantiate this statement. He claims that when he saw the teamster coming with such a formidable looking weapon he thought it was about time to give up and so he had pulled out his revolver for the purpose of handing it over when the blamed thing went off, placing him in a very embarrassing position .

When the five were practically cornered and the only thing left for them to do was to fight it out, they gave up. The sight of Libby's Winchester probably having considerable to do with influencing them to surrender.

"We's lost and you fellows have won," one of them called out as they put up their hands, while Dixon and Ryan handed over their guns. The others were searched, but no weapons were found on them and then they were taken back to the village on a horse sled. Postmaster Rich and his men had nothing to bind them with, but having got their revolvers and being armed themselves they did not fear that they would make an attempt to escape.

HAD POSTAGE STAMPS

During the chase through the woods, one of the yeggs threw away a box containing a lot of postage

stamps and this was afterwards found in the snow by a man named **Bonnett**.

The news of the capture quickly spread throughout the town of Standish and other nearby communities and Sheriff Moulton was first notified by **Albert H. Butterfield**, the town clerk and treasurer and proprietor of a general store at Standish Village. The sheriff got the message about five o'clock and if he and Deputy Sheriff Harmon didn't do some hustling, then nobody ever did. As soon as they could get ready they started for the Union Station to catch the train over the mountain division of the Maine Central railroad. On the way to the station, they fell in with somebody who had an automobile and jumping into this they managed to just reach the train before it pulled out. And they went to Sebago Lake, got the prisoners, and came back on the train that reaches Portland at eight o'clock. Isn't that going some? As soon as they reached the lake, Sheriff Moulton telephoned to the United States Marshal's office and he also notified the morning papers of the capture.

TOWN EXCITED

The yeggs were in the railroad station at Sebago Lake when the Sheriff and Deputy Harmon got there, and the waiting room was packed with people while a big crowd numbering little less than 200 people was gathering outside. A good many of the folks were armed, too, 'tis said for they didn't intend to take the slightest chance of the strangers getting away. Sheriff Moulton and Deputy Harmon, after notifying various people of the round-up, including Sheriff **Charles O. Emery** of York county, and looking about a little and hearing the story of the four men who effected the capture, were ready to return to the city. They handcuffed the yeggs securely and when they put them aboard the train the crowd at the lake station began to melt away.

News that the men had been taken was spread all over this city within a very short time after it reached the sheriff's office, and so, when the

Sebago Lake Station

train from up country pulled in, there was a big crowd at the Union Station. United States Deputy Marshall **Burton M. Smith** and Post Office inspector **Spofford** were among those to arrive and Deputy Sheriff **Harry B. Hartford**, whose home is in Standish, was also there. The prisoners were hustled into a couple of hacks and it wasn't long before they were landed in jail.

THE NAMES GIVEN

There they gave their names as follows: **Harry C. Morgan** of Wales, **John T. Ryan** of Berlin N.H., **Fred R. Dixon** of Canada and **George Sullivan** of New York. All of them appeared to be between the ages of 30 and 40, and Ryan was the heaviest one of the lot. On the whole, they were tough looking customers. It is understood that they made statements which lead the officers to believe they are the ones who broke into the West Buxton post office and the box of stamps that was found would be pretty good evidence, even if they had said nothing. After they had emptied their pockets and had been stripped, two pairs of shoes were found to have rubber on them. Rubber and other articles were

Harry B Hartford

taken from the store of **Warren A. McCorrison** at West Buxton.

PLAYED THE GAME

It is said, that on the way to Portland, one of the men said that they had played the game to the limit and lost. On Dixon, when his pockets were turned inside out was a money bag that has been identified as one used by postmasters for keeping their change. He claimed when it was found on him that he had had it for seven years.

Deputy United States Marshal Smith came to the jail with the other officers and he took the men's names. He will probably investigate the case more fully today, and the men will be arraigned in the United States court for breaking and entering the post office.

Of course everybody was delighted that the quintet had been captured and the four men who did the trick are having all sorts of nice things said

about them for their exhibition of pluck. There was a rumor last night that Libby was so incensed when Rosborough was shot that he wanted to open fire on the desperadoes with his rifle, but he didn't have to, for they came down from their perch right away.

THE BUXTON ROBBERY

When the West Buxton post office was entered. and the safe blown, from $50 to $100 worth of stamps and cash were taken and at the McCorrison store new rubbers were taken and the old ones left in the street. The other place visited was the dry goods store of **John Berryman**, a traveling man in the employ of the Clark-Eddy Co. of this city and there the cash drawer was rifled. The morning after the breaks, **Oscar D. Rand**, who lives about a mile and a half from West Buxton on the Bar Mills road, found that his horse was missing and later in the day the team was found standing in the road about four miles above West Buxton on the road leading to Sebago Lake. When questioned about the team last night, the five men who were taken into custody strenuously denied having taken it.

Some suspects were searched at Sebago Lake the day following the burglaries but they were allowed to go up the line on the 9:20 train. Later, the York county officials were not satisfied and so an officer went up the line and searched them again at North Conway. Nothing could be found on them, though, and so, once more, they were released. They had been employed cutting ice at the lake.

Portland Evening Express & Advertiser - Monday, January 29, 1912

*There were two **Alexander Rossborough**'s at that time, father and son, both living in Scarborough. Alexander, the father, was 71 in 1912 and died in 1913 of dementia. Alexander W., the son, was 21. Most likely it was this Alexander that was involved in the shooting. Alexander W. died in 1974 in Biddeford.*

Dear Aunt Nellie,

Just got your letter, yes I had a pretty close call. I don't care to try it again. We got those fellows about 3 1/2 miles from here toward No. Gorham in the woods beyond Chadbourne's. Uncle Lewis will know pretty near. Chase them down a logging road for about (from our house up to Crockett's). When we came up to them in a place where they had dragged out logs, there Libby and I waited for them. Lem was right. Me and the fellow that done the shooting was ahead, he passed Lem and Libby, and I took him and he had his hands in his pockets and stopped him and asked him to take his hand out of his pockets. When he did, he made a grab for my gun with his right and stepped back just a little and fired at me but I threw back my head and the bullet did not hit me - when he fired Rosborough jumped and grabbed him and in the scrap he fired twice again - one going through Ross- right lung. Harry Paine and I both jumped for his gun but

Paine was ahead of me. Lem and Libby had the other four in a line where they had drug out log. Libby saw the big fellow's gun sticking out of his pocket so, he put the muzzle of his rifle right in his face, the fellow kinder warded it off and when he did, Libby reached over and took his gun. This happened before the shooter and if it hadn't, possibly some of us would have got hurt because this would have given the rest of them courage.

The next day, we found a gun where we took them, so, they had three and we think two more. They had plenty of cartridges.

The choppers that are working for Mr. Roberts found two bags of money, a box of stamps, and stamp boxes, and a watch, and the gun.

They are starting a paper for the fellow that got hurt so to pay his expense in the hospital. There is a standing reward for of $200 a head that means if we get it $200 a piece hope we do, especially Rosborough. This is a standard reward from the Government.

The Press had the right account of it and you watch the Press they sent out for our pictures. I have not got any only some Eva has taken.

Well it is most mail time and I shall have to get busy as Lem has gone to Portland. Come up when you can. Give Eva's and my love to all the folk.

Asa

This is written in a hurry.

A Letter from Asa Douglass to his Aunt Nellie

Douglass Files

Asa Martin Douglass at this time was living in Sebago Lake Village, third house on the right from the intersection on what is now called Chadbourne rd. At the time of this event, his wife, Geneva Libby Douglass was eight months pregnant with their first child, Lloyd - my father.

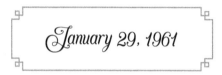

January 29, 1961

The R. G. Johnson Bat Shop burned. The fire started around a chimney in the attic. Bats made by Rupert Johnson were cherished by his players and sought after by major league professionals, many of which made the trek to Maine to visit the shop for a custom bat.

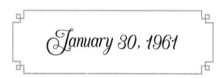

January 30, 1961

The Steep Falls railroad station was burned as an exercise by the Standish Fire Department. The building, built in 1870, contained a dance hall and stage. It was replaced by a feed and grain store.

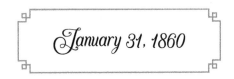

FROM THE DIARY OF JOHN P. MOULTON

Warm in the fore noon, afternoon cold and windy and snowed in the afternoon. Father started for Biddeford about two o'clock afternoon. **Simon** and **Irvin Libby** went over to the fall (Steep Falls) with logs. Hauled home boards. I worked in the shop.

STANDISH, MAINE

EST

FEBRUARY

1785

CUMBERLAND COUNTY

Lemuel Rich retired as Postmaster in Sebago Lake Village after 38 years. He was appointed in 1904 by President Theodore Roosevelt. Son of **John H. Rich**, he was born in 1876 at the store on the corner of Routes 35 and 25, a grocery and general merchandise store that also contained the Post Office. That store today is Walker's Landing, a sandwich shop.

Mail Room at Rich's Store abt 1910

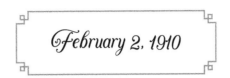

FROM THE STATE OF MAINE AGRICULTURAL DEPARTMENT IN AUGUSTA TO MR. LEWIS M. MOULTON, CHAIRMAN OF THE BOARD OF SELECTMEN:

My dear Sir:

I have received your letter of January 27th, and note what you say in relation to removing the brown-tail moth nests from the beautiful elm trees. All care should be exercised not to mar their beauty. In some sections, people have shot the nests off without any serious injury to the tree, but as far as I could I would remove them with clippers. These can be procured and attached to a long pole, and a young man by going up into the tree with this pole could probably reach most of the nests. The few that are left might be taken off by shooting without any special injury to the tree, if proper care is exercised...

Respectfully yours, **A. W. Gilman**

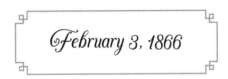

TO THE OVERSEERS OF THE POOR OF THE TOWN OF STANDISH

Gentlemen, You are hereby notified that **Lorenzo Decker** and **Sarah A. Decker**, his wife, have fallen into distress, and stand in need of immediate relief, in the town of Baldwin, which has been furnished by said town of Baldwin, on the account and proper charge of the Town of Standish, where they have their legal settlement. You are requested to remove said paupers to the Town of Standish, accordingly, and to defray the expense of their support in the town of Baldwin, amounting to about seventeen or eighteen dollars to date, including doctor bill of about seven or eight dollars. **D. F. Richardson**, one of the overseers of the poor of the Town of Baldwin.

I have been talking with the doctor. He thinks Decker's wife will probably get better in the course of one or two weeks. She has had the inflammatory fever, and doesn't well, fast.

Expense now five dollars per week, besides doctoring.

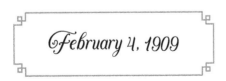

FROM THE DIARY OF GILBERT MOULTON OF SEBAGO LAKE VILLAGE

Pleasant and cold, was on the route until 3-15 PM, around home rest of day and evening, **Daniel Ward** was buried today. **Frank H. Rands** building burned this morning. They saved all the household goods and his stock.

Steep Falls, Mr. **Higgins**, Dear Sir, I have got through with the **Skillings** family at last. There was three of the children had the Diphtheria one after another, and the wonder is that they did not all die in the dirt and filth together or get knocked over in some of the rows. I looked after them as well as I could and left them as soon as I thought it safe to do so. I got off with only sixteen visits but it was the most disagreeable place I've visited for a long time. Did you get a bill from me for my attendance last spring on a **Kelley** family that belonged to Bridgton. I sent it to you but never heard from it after. Also, for a boy that belonged to Limerick who got hurt in the hotel stable last spring. The bill was given to **Andrew Ridlon** to carry to you. He said, you said that we must take care of the boy and the town would pay the bill, but as I have not received any pay for these cases I would like to know about it so, I called to see you once but you was away. Please let me hear from you about the matter or call if agreeable to you soon.

Yours, **J BB. Andrews M.D.**

FROM THE STATE OF MAINE EMERGENCY RELIEF ADMINISTRATION TO WILBERT A. LIBBY, CHAIRMAN OF THE BOARD OF SELECTMEN

Following is a list of boys from your town who have been assigned for the C.C.C. Camps - **Stuart W. Hooper** & **Roland Philip Lewis**.

The Civilian Conservation Corps was a voluntary work program for Unemployed, unmarried men ages 17-28. Operating from 1933 to 1942, the program supplied jobs for young men during the Great Depression.

Stuart Hooper

Roland Lewis

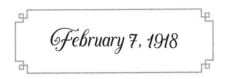

February 7, 1918

FROM THE AUTOGRAPH BOOK OF GEORGIE HIGGINS

Fruits grow old as soon as they ripen,
Love and Kisses soon grows cold,
Young men's vows are soon forgotten,
Look out Georgie and don't get sold.

Your friend, **Edna Waterman**

Georgie Evilin Higgins *was born December 19, 1897 to* **John M. and Alice Shurtfeff Higgins** *in Sebago Lake and died in December 1982 in Westbrook at 85. In 1924 she married* **William P. Allen.** *At the time of this writing, she was 21 years old.*

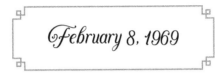

February 8, 1969

Standish, and the rest of Maine, got hit by a Nor'easter. Across the next three days the storm dropped 50 inches of snow.

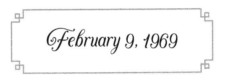

February 9, 1969

The second day of the storm, In Steep Falls, Route 113 became impassible due to a snow drift reportedly 300 yards long and 17 feet deep in some places. It was cleared

The accompanying photo is not that snow drift and not from that storm but gives some perspective to the size.

Samuel Small, an employee of the Androscoggin Pulp Company, had the two middle fingers on his right hand cut off up to the first joint while at work on the pressure pump. He is getting along as well as expected.

—Portland Press Herald

Pulp Mill - Steep Falls

February, 11, 1867

The Portland and Ogdensburg Railroad was incorporated. It was to run a line from Portland to Ogdensburg NY through Sebago Lake village, Richville, and Steep Falls.

Portland & Ogdensburg Railroad at Sebago Lake Station 1870

February 12, 1839

A Town Warrant was issued "To see what course the Town will take in relation to the petition of **Daniel Fogg** to be set off from Standish to Gorham—together with twenty acres of land—as per order of Notice from the Senate & House of Representatives of February 7, 1839, in Maine.

February 13, 1842

Dear Grandmother,

I have been thinking about writing you a letter. School finished yesterday and I think I shall be over pretty soon to make a long visit. Mother is going to write a letter to Uncle Stephen to-day and send it by to-morrow. I am not very well. I have a bad cold and a sore mouth. Father has not finished his singing school, yet, he has got to keep two or three weeks more. Marcia Came(??) is very well indeed. Aunt Dorcas is married and moved away. I have got a new book to read at school and it is called the Worcester Fourth Book. We did not go to meeting to-day because it was so muddy. I have been through my Arithmetic twice since school began. Marcia Anna went to school last Friday. Mother has been cracking walnuts and eating of them and she got the shells all over the floor. I am going to foot Mother a pair of cotton stocking. Tuesday afternoon. I am knitting edging to sell to Sarah. I am not so well to-day as it was Sabbath day and I expect that I have taken cold and have been quite sick for a few days. When Father came home last week he brought us a quart of Walnuts. Mother says that I must not write but once about the same thing at all, but I forgot that I mentioned walnuts before. I cannot write anymore because I expect Mr. Mitchell along every minute, so good-bye from your loving granddaughter,

Lucinda Paine

(Sent to Mrs. Anna Otis, Limington)

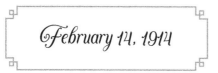

February 14, 1914

J. L. Swasey, H.W. Dow, Henry Nelson, Charles Mason, Henry Stone, L. B. Whitney, Earl P. Brooks and **Reginald Lowell** were each paid by the town of Standish three dollars for gathering Brown Tail Moth Nests.

Howard Dow

Linwood Whitney

Reginald Lowell

February 15, 1864

A warrant was issued to the inhabitants of Standish "to determine whether said town will raise a sum of money not exceeding twenty five dollars for each man of its proportion of troops required by the President of the United States under the call of February 1, 1864 to be used in paying recruiting agents and other expenses of enlistment." and, "to determine whether said town will raise by loan a sum of money. ... for paying to its recruits under aforesaid call a bounty - not to exceed three hundred dollars to each recruit to be reimbursed to said town by the State under the provisions of the statute..."

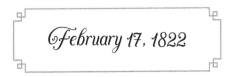

February 16, 1784

COMMONWEALTH OF MASSACHUSETTS, IN SENATE, FEBRUARY 14, 1784

Resolved, That the committee for examining and settling the Accounts of the late Treasurer Gardner, be, and they are hereby directed to carry out in Specie the balance due from several towns, as contained in the representation made by said committee to the General Court, in their present sessions, eliminating such balances, and give immediate notice to such towns as shall appear to be delinquent, and to issue his execution against the collectors of such of the said towns as shall neglect or delay to pay into the treasurer, their respective balances, within three months after Notice given as aforesaid. - Sent down for concurrence, Samuel Adams, President

In the House of Representatives, February 16, 1784, Read and Concurred, Tristam Dalton, Speaker. Approved, John Hancock - On the back of the document, written - Town of Pearsontown, Taxes for 1776-77-78-79 & 80 - £445..19.2 (445 Pounds, 19 Shillings, 2 Pence)

This resolution was met by surprise and alarm by Pearsontown taxpayers as they were not aware of this delinquency. £445 for five years of back taxes was an enormous sum for this community. Tax Collectors would be jailed and their houses, contents, and lands would be sold to recover this money. At that time, tax collectors signed an oath to be responsible for the money they would collect and were paid a percentage of the collection when they turned the money in to the town treasurer. Needless to say that the town immediately appealed to the House of Representatives of Massachusetts and relief was granted.

February 17, 1822

TO THE CLERK OF THE TOWN OF STANDISH:

Found in the highway in Standish between the Carrying Place & Wescott's bridge—a small French silver watch with a brass chain—dated on the inside.

James Thomes.

The "Carrying Place" was the area around the intersection of routes 35 and 237, also known as Chadbourne's Landing. Wescott's bridge is probably the bridge from Standish to North Windham on Route 35.

Canal Bridge on Chadbourne Rd (Route 35) 1985

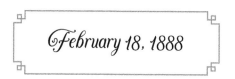

February 18, 1888

A warrant was issued for a March 5th Town Meeting, among other things:

"To see if the town will vote to raise a sum of money to be used towards furnishing free textbooks for the scholars in the public schools.

"To see if they will vote to act in conjunction with the town of Windham in putting an iron bridge over the Presumpscot river and raising money therefore:

"To see if the town will vote to let the band have the use of the town hall free for practicing."

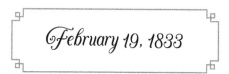

February 19, 1833

TO OLIVER FROST, TOWN TREASURER OR HIS SUCCESSOR:

Pays **Phineas Ingalls** twenty dollars it for vaccination of the inhabitants of Standish. Selectmen of Standish: **Benjamin Poland, Benjamin Chadbourne, Jabez Dow**

Edward Jenner *is usually credited with developing the smallpox vaccine and vaccination procedure;* *however forms of vaccination had existed for centuries. He did, however, elevate the procedure to scientific levels. The first vaccination against smallpox was probably* **Benjamin Jesty** *who used cowpox material to vaccinate. The procedure was to inoculate using a lancet to "prick" the skin on the arms.*

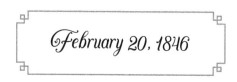

February 20, 1846

FROM THE STORE LEDGER OF GARDNER DENNETT

William Marean was hired to pick up supplies in Portland. He hauled:

- 1 hogshead of Molasses
- 1 barrel Whiskey
- 1 barrel Pork
- 88 lbs. Tea
- 14 - 30 lbs. candles
- 400 lbs. Fish.

A hogshead of Molasses was about 79 gallons, a Barrel of Whiskey was 53 gallons.

The Steep Falls Baptist Church celebrated its 90th anniversary. The program consisted of the church service, a historical sketch of local society by **Guy Sanborn**, a history of the church in living pictures, and a History of the Church by Mrs. **Eunice Mayo**.

BAPTIST CHURCH, STEEP FALLS, ME. 6.

The Sebago Lake Regional Parish along with the public schools of the Parish hosted a Winter Carnival at Otter Ponds. There were Cross Country ski races, Snowshoe dash, a three legged ski dash, ski jumps, skating races including a backward skate race, and more. In the evening, at the High School, there were two one act plays and the crowning of the King and Queen.

1927 Winter Carnival

1927 Winter Carnival

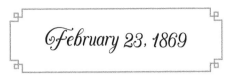

February 23, 1869

The Maine House of Representatives passed "An Act to set off part of the Town of Standish and annex the same to the Town of Raymond." Raymond Cape once was Standish Cape. The Act was passed by the Senate the next day.

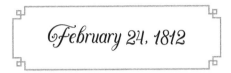

February 24, 1812

A wild cat came to a window at **Eleazer Parker's** House, which lighted a room wherein three of his daughters were in bed. Leaping against the window sash which Eleazer heard, and thinking it was a cat that formerly been a domestic of the family, he called to one of his daughters to open the window to the cat to prevent her from breaking the glass. Scarcely had he spoken, when the cat, redoubling her strength, burst through a pane of glass into the room, and, from the table, leaped upon the bed, seizing the eldest girl by the nose, who cried to her father that the cat would kill her. He instantly sprung out of bed; ran into the room and caught the animal by one of her hind legs and drew her from the girl and bed. However, in his effort, the cat biting him thro' the arm, he was obliged to break his hold. Opening a door, he let in his dog, who began to run upon the cat but she resisted with such violence that it compelled the dog to retreat. By this time, Eleazer had lighted a candle, and immediately the cat grew timid and sought to hide under the bed clothes and soon fell easy prey to Eleazer. About three weeks after this, the girl bitten was taken ill, and a physician being sent for, on presenting a cup of water to her, immediately discovered her disease, Hydrophobia (Rabies), to be occasioned by the bite of the cat. Six days after which, she died; and later, her father, feeling uncommonly disordered, sent for his family physician, who declared him in the same condition that his daughter was in.

From an unknown newspaper obituary

The house was located at the intersection of Thomas Rd and the Pond Road. The cat was most probably a Bobcat.

Standish Ministerial Lands Sec. 1, Be it enacted by the Senate and House of Representatives, in General Court assembled, and by the authority of the same, that deacon **Jonathan Philbrick**, Mr. **Bryan Martin**, **Edward Tompson**, **Daniel Cram Jun.** and **John Sanborn**, the trustees named in an act, entitled "An act authorizing the sale of part of the Ministerial Lands in the first parish in the Town of Standish," passed the twenty-fifth day of February, in the year one thousand and eight hundred and twelve be, and they hereby are authorized to sell and convey, in fee simple, the thirty acre lot, whereon the meeting-house stands in said town, (excepting and reserving out of the north west corner of said lot, one half acre of land to be laid out ten rods fronting on the main road and to extend back eight rods, whereon the matting-house stands)...

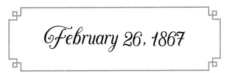

February 26, 1867

The Portland Water Company received permission to take water from Sebago Lake.

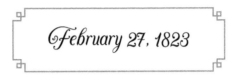

February 27, 1823

Pursuant to a town warrant, the town voted, among other things, "To restrain cattle and horses from running at large within such limits as the town sees fit."

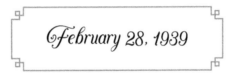

February 28, 1939

Ina (Shaw Wescott) slipped and fell on the icy platform at the Sebago Lake Station and broke her ankle in two places. Sent to the State Street Hospital the same day. Came home the 11th of March, her leg in a cast. Will have to wear it six weeks or more.

Ina Louise Shaw Wescott, born in 1889, was 50 at the time of this accident. While the Standish Historical Society does not have a photo of Ina at that age, It does have one of Ina as a baby, shown below.

The roof of Wildwood, a popular Dance Hall, Pavilion and Roller Skating rink in Steep Falls collapsed under the weight of snow. The venue was extremely popular with teens at Standish High and surrounding schools. The building was rebuilt.

March 2, 1835

A warrant was issued for a town meeting for the town to vote, among other things, "To restrain cattle from running at large within such limits as the town may think proper." This was a recurring issue that appeared in many early town warrants.

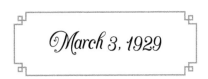

March 3, 1929

Fred Cole, the Town Clerk and Treasurer paid a total of $23.25 for the years of 1927, 1928 to March 2, 1929 Porcupine Bounty.

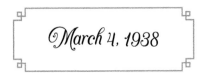

March 4, 1938

A 16 room hotel and stable in Steep Falls owned by postmaster **Frank L. Strout** burned. It was a complete loss. Below, on the right is the Strout hotel.

Steep Falls, Me.

March 5, 1783

An article appeared in the town warrant to clear a road to Sebago Lake. This would be the construction of what is now Northeast road.

The Annual Report for the year ending February 15, 1911 Article 21 was "To see if the town will vote to buy one or more Chemical Fire Engines, and raise money for the same." The vote was held on March 6, 1911.

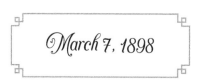

March 7, 1898

W. M. Libby (Willie Marrett Libby) was paid one dollar and 24 cents "being for cash paid for use of the telegraph and telephone." Libby was a selectman of the town and was being reimbursed.

March 8, 1786

COMMONWEALTH OF MASSACHUSETTS: SENATE:

On the petition of **Jonathan Philbrick** & others, shewing that they were by the Court of General Sessions of the peace for the County of Cumberland, appointed assessors & collectors of taxes for the plantation called Pearsontown. It were severally notified by one of the justices for the peace, for the same County, to appear before him to take the oaths to qualify them for the aforesaid offices of assessors & collectors; that they the petitioners are much embarrassed, finding that if they should take the oaths aforesaid, it would be their duty to assess & collect all the taxes that have been ordered to be assessed on the aforesaid plantation ever since their first settlement (being more than twenty years) which the petitioners apprehend will be impracticable for them to execute with any tolerable degree of equity, and that the whole amount will be much beyond the ability of the inhabitants to pay, - and praying the consideration of this court.

Resolved that the inhabitants of the said plantation, lately known by the name of Pearsontown, now incorporated into a town by the name of Standish, be helot pay the sum of five hundred pounds only, in discharge of the whole of the several taxes laid upon the said plantation, previous to their incorporation aforesaid -

And be it further resolved, that the aforesaid petitioners after severally taking the oaths required by law to qualify them for their respective offices of Assessors & Collectors as aforesaid, shall be excused from paying the whole or any part of the penalty, which by law they were subjected to, by neglecting to take the oaths of their respective offices, when required then to, provided they shall take such oath respectively on or before the fifteenth day of April next, any law to the contrary notwithstanding -

And be it further resolved, that the aforesaid assessors be, & they hereby are directed to assess the aforesaid sum of five hundred pounds on the polls and estates of the inhabitants of the said Town of Standish, agreeably to the rules & directions in the last Tax Act made & provided. And the same assessment commit to a Collector or Collectors for the Town aforesaid & certify to the Treasurer of this Commonwealth, their doings & the summer sums so assessed & committed to a Collector or Collectors, on or before the last day of May next.

Sent down for concurrence — **Samuel Phillips Junior**, President

In the House of Representatives March 8th, 1786, Read & concurred **A. Ward**, Speaker

Approved, **James Bowdoin** — True Copy attest — **John Avery Jr.**, Secretary

March 9, 1864

New Gloucester, Gents:

We notified you some time since that **Israel Thorn**, wife & child had become chargeable in our town and a legal inhabitant of your town. We need a letter of denial, and upon inquiry we find that his legal residence is in your town. First, he lived with **David Allen** until he was twenty one years old and since then there is no time that he has lived in New Gloucester two years since he has an acct book, where he has kept his acct with every man he worked for since that time. We thought we would let you know the particulars about the case so you might think the matter over and if you think best to settle the bill without making needly cost you can do so. You know these lawyers show no mercy when they get to work for towns. Please let us know what you will do soon.

Respectfully yours, **D. W. Merrill**, Secretary of the Board of Overseers N. G.

N. B. the amount due is thirty seven 50/100 dollars. If you think it best to settle the bill, you can send it by mail and we will send you a receipt for the same.

March 10, 1984

Article to be Voted by Secret Ballot – Article 2A. To see if the town will vote to authorize the Selectmen to withdraw a sum of money from surplus to purchase a computer; that sum being thirty thousand dollars.

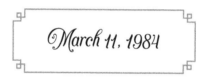

March 11, 1984

The referendum on whether to purchase a computer system was turned down, 256-217.

Thus the entry of Standish into the world of technology was delayed over fears that this "bandwagon" was just a flash in the pan and the technology untried.

March 12, 1819

The great snowstorm of 1819 began about 4 o'clock in the afternoon and continued for three days during which time about four feet of snow fell, which were piled into enormous drifts by high winds that blew over the last two days of the storm. During this storm, **Mr. and Mrs. Tarbox** who lived on Standish Cape, now Raymond Cape, perished in the storm. The event was memorialized by the Standish Poet **Thomas Shaw** in his 40 verse broadside, "Mournful Song" and noted in a letter from the writer **Nathaniel Hawthorne** to his uncle. Hawthorne claimed the storm lasted nine days. It might have, he was there. To the right is an image of the Thomas Shaw broadside which memorialized the event. (Poem at right)

MOURNFUL SONG

on a man and wife, who both froze to death in one night, on Standish Cape, so called.

By Thomas Shaw of Standish Maine

1 Attend my soul and hear the sound,
That's solemnly a passing round,
That strikes each heart and listening ear
To hear the solemn sound draw near.

2 Husbands and wives may now attend,
And let your hearts to heaven ascend,
While I unto you do make known,
A solemn-stroke as e'er was born.

3 Let children too draw round and hear
With trembling hearts and holy fear,
With all our neighbours all as one
And listen till my story's done.

4 And thou great God pray lead my heart
And mind to act my solemn part,
In this affair before our eyes,
Which stricketh all hearts with surprise.

5 Good Lord confound every one
Who ever to these lines make fun,
That they may hide their heads with shame,
Or brought to praise thy holy name.

6 And now the story I shall tell,
Who am informed of it full well,
And O my soul what can this mean
A real or a fancied dream.

7 O yes it is the truth I tell,
On Standish Cape these two did dwell,
Together liv'd as man and wife,
Until ended their day of life.

MOURNFUL SONG,

On a man and wife, who both froze to death in
one night, on Standish Cape, so called.

1
Attend my soul and hear the sound,
That's solemnly a passing round,
That strikes each heart and listening ear
To hear the solemn sound draw near.

2
Husbands and wives may now attend,
And let your hearts to heaven ascend,
While I unto you do make known,
A solemn-stroke as e'er was born.

3
Let children too draw round and hear
With trembling hearts and holy fear,
With all our neighbours all as one
And listen till my story's done.

4
And thou great God pray lead my heart
And mind to act my solemn part,
In this affair before our eyes,
Which stricketh all hearts with surprise.

5
Good Lord confound every one
Who ever to these lines make fun,
That they may hide their heads with shame,
Or brought to praise thy holy name.

6
And now the story I shall tell,
Who am informed of it full well,
And O my soul what can this mean
A real or a fancied dream.

7
O yes it is the truth I tell,
On Standish Cape these two did dwell,
Together liv'd as man and wife,
Until ended their day of life.

8
This man for food abroad did go,
In a snow-storm in a deep snow,
At his return, his strength gave way,
Which brought him to his dying day.

9
Under his load he seemed to fall,
And then aloud for help did call,
His wife his dying sound did hear
Then for his help did soon repair.

10
She left her children then with speed
To help her husband then in need,
Through cold and wind in a deep snow,
God knows what she did undergo.

11
She met her husband in a fright
Through winds and snow on a cold night,
Whom . . . . own
To save his life she lost her own.

12
She took her clothes from off her frame,
And on her husband plac'd the same,
For help she cried aloud and strong
Was her last fierce and mournful song.

13
O there she tended on her man
When he could neither go nor stand,
And when lain out upon the snow,
God knows what she did undergo.

14
Dead or alive we cannot tell,
God only knows the scene full well,
And her great cries that God would save
Her husband from the gaping grave.

15
Trouble and grief, sorrow and woe,
. . . .
There nurs'd her husband in the cold,
Which makes our child's blood run cold.

16
We cannot tell, nor can we show,
To others what we do not know,
But this we say a doleful night,
Upon this man and wife did light.

17
Without a covering or a bed
That woman then in doleful dread,
Tended her man in cold and snow,
God knows what they did undergo.

18
Tempestuous winds and storm of snow
About this man and wife did blow,
Distress'd in body and in mind
This woman thought some help to find.

19
Her husband to God did steer,
So then for help she steer'd her ways,
With solemn groans ascending high
While her poor children heard her cry.

20
Soon feeble woman took her flight
For help upon this doleful night,
For help she sought, for help she cried,
Where human help was then denied.

21
Towards her neighbors she did steer
Through snow and wind and doleful fear,
With solemn cries that God would save
Her, and mercy upon her have.

22
She went as long as she could stand,
Aiming for human help at hand,
With bitter groans and solemn cries
That therefore the Lord arise.

23
And then she crept upon all four,
Until her clothes from her were tore,
The snow flying—sorrow and woe,
God only knew her trouble too.

24
Her solemn cries arose on high
Her children hearing of her cry,
Which did distress each thoughtful mind,
While they could not their parent find.

25
Their Father lying in the snow,
Their Mother for help tried to go,
Creeping and crying as she went
Until her life was almost spent.

26
She crept till to a bloody gore,
Her flesh was into pieces tore,
And only knew her heart-felt cries,
Which did unto the heavens arise.

27
Until at last gave up her race,
And her self too, to sovereign grace,
And with her doleful cries severe,
Which reached to her Saviour's ear.

28
Her cries we say to heaven arose,
Then did her troubled heart compose,
What time it was we cannot tell,
She bid her troubles all farewell.

29
And there she died, her husband too,
Both of them parish'd in the snow,
And gone to rest we humble trust,
As all good people surely must.

30
Two days these children were alone,
Their absent parents to bemoan,
That God above did hear their cry,
When both these parents quick did die.

31
A neighbour then on the third day,
Towards these children took his way,
To his surprise he looking around
A helpless corps upon the ground.

32
Looking about he saw also,
Her husband dead upon the snow,
With a surprise on them did look,
Then to the children he partook.

33
The solemn tidings to them told,
While their great grief they could not hold,
Which was full sore to every one,
As if those youths were all undone.

34
To them it was a doleful day,
Both of their parents took away,
Which caused their tender hearts to bleed,
When they did want a friend indeed.

35
Thus they were left—their parents there
Were buried decently by men,
A solemn sound to fly abroad
All over ruled by a God.

36
God bless those children in distress,
That are Father and Motherless,
Till the affliction that they have,
Shall be a means their souls to save.

37
Grand parents of those little ones
God make them his daughters and son,
And may you live to bless God's name
While in a sinful world of fame.

38
God bless the people all around
That heareth of this doleful sound,
Prepare us all by sea and land
To meet all troubles fresh at hand.

39
Thousands of people good Lord save,
Made of materials for the grave,
So thy great name shall have the praise,
Sounding by many means and ways.

40
Have mercy Lord on sinful man,
And kindly lengthen out his span,
Which shall glory and honor bring
To Christ the universal King.

8 This man for food abroad did go
   In a snow-storm in a deep snow,
   At his return his strength gave way,
   Which brought him to his dying day.

9 Under his load he seemed to fall,
   And then aloud for help did call,
   His wife his dying sound did hear
   Then for his help did soon repair.

10 She left her children then with speed
   To help her husband then in need,
   Through cold and wind in a deep snow,
   God knows what she did undergo.

11 She met her husband in a fright
   Through winds and snow on a cold night,
   Whom she most lovingly did own
   To save his life she lost her own.

12 She took her clothes from off her frame
   And on her husband plac'd the same,
   For help she cried aloud and strong
   Was her last fierce and mournful song.

13 O there she tended on her man
   When he could neither go nor stand,
   And when lain out upon thes now,
   God knows what she did undergo.

14 Dead or alive we cannot tell,
   God only knows the scene full well,
   And her great cries that God would save
   Her husband from the gapeing grave.

15 Trouble and grief, sorrow and woe,
   This good woman did undergo,
   There nurs'd her husband in the cold,
   Which makes our chill'd blood run cold.

16 We cannot tell, nor can-we show,
   To others what we do not know,
   But this we say a doleful night,
   Upon this man and wife did light.

17 Without a covering or a bed
   That woman then in doleful dread,
   Tended her man in cold and snow,
   God knows what they did undergo.

18 Tempestuous winds and storm of snow
   About this man and wife did blow,
   Distress'd in body and in mind
   This woman thought some help to find.

19 Her husband to God did convey,
   So then for help she steer'd her way,
   With solemn groans ascending high
   While her poor children heard her cry.

20 Soon feeble woman took her flight
   For help upon this doleful night,
   For help she sought, for help she cried,
   Where human help was then denied.

21 Towards her neighbors she did steer
   Through snow and wind and doleful fear,
   With solemn cries that God would save
   Her, and mercy upon her have.

22 She went as long as she could stand,
   Aiming for human help at hand,
   With bitter groans and solemn cries
   That did before the Lord arise.

23 And then she crept upon all four,
   Until her clothes from her were tore,
   The snow flying—sorrow and woe,
   God only knew her trouble too.

24 Her solemn cries arose on high
   Her children hearing of her cry,
   Which did distress each thoughtful mind,
   While they could not their parent find.

25 Their Father lying in the snow,
   Their Mother for help tried to go,
   Creeping and crying as she went
   Until her life was almost spent.

26 She crept till to a bloody gore,
    Her flesh was into pieces tore,
    God only knew her heart-felt cries,
    Which did unto the heavens arise.

27 Until at last gave up her race,
    And her self too, to sovereign grace,
    And with her doleful cries severe,
    Which reached to her Saviours ear.

28 Her cries we say to heaven arose,
    Then did her troubled heart compose,
    What time it was we cannot tell,
    She bid her troubles all farewell.

29 And there she died, her husband too,
    Both of them perish'd in the snow,
    And gone to rest we humble trust,
    As all good people surely must.

30 Two days these children were alone,
    Their absent parents to bemoan,
    That God above did hear their cry,
    When both these parents quick did die.

31 A neighbour then on the third day,
    Towards these children took his way,
    To his surprise the woman found
    A helpless corps upon the ground.

32 Looking about he saw also,
    Her husband dead upon the snow,
    With a surprise on them did look,
    Then to the children he partook.

33 The solemn tidings to them told,
    While their great grief they could not hold,
    Which was full sore to every one,
    As if those youths were all undone.

34 To them it was a doleful day,
    Both of their parents took away,
    Which caused their tender hearts to bleed,
    When they did want a friend indeed.

35 Thus they were left—their parents then
    Were buried decently by men,
    A solemn sound to fly abroad
    All over rulled by a God.

36 God bless those children in distress,
    That are Father and Motherless,
    Till the affliction that they have,
    Shall be a means their souls to save.

37 Grand parents of those little ones
    God make them his daughters and son,
    And may you live to bless God's name
    While in a sinful world of fame.

38 God bless the people all around
    That heareth of this doleful sound,
    Prepare us all by sea and land
    To meet all troubles fresh at hand.

39 Thousands of people good Lord save,
    Made of materials for the grave,
    So thy great name shall have the praise,
    Sounding by many means and ways.

40 Have mercy Lord on sinful man,
    And kindly lengthen out his span,
    Which shall glory and honor bring
    To Christ the universal King.

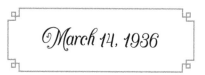

March 13, 1813

Daniel Shaw, son of **Thomas Shaw** the poet, wrote in his diary: "Went to **Eleazer Parker**'s funeral. Mr. Parker and a daughter of his was bit by a mad wildcat a year ago, which came into his house in the night. The daughter made an outcry that the cat was biting her; he got up and drove the cat out of the house and in the scrape the cat bit him. The daughter died a month or two afterwards. He lived until this month; he had a terrible sickness; was in great pain some days before he died. Many went to see him. **Elder Leach** preached his funeral sermon, and a great many people attended and it was a solemn time."

See February 24. Parker's home was located at the intersection of Thomas Rd and the Pond Rd.

March 14, 1936

At the Gorham Normal School Tourney, despite that Gorham, Berwick Academy and Kennebunk were the favorites, Standish brought home the Championship Trophy. They beat Kennebunk 44-26 in the first round, Scarborough in the Semifinals, and avenged two regular season defeats with Gorham, beating them in the Champions game 34-27.

1936 Crimson Rambler

*The 1936 Basketball team, under the leadership of Coach **Rupert Johnson**, had a 14 win 3 loss record for the season. Captain **Nelson Carver** is holding the Russell Trophy.*

Coach Rupert Johnson — Frederick Rand — Raymond Edgecomb — Robert Graffam — Manager Elliot Hubbard

Francis Ettinger — Corey Snowden — Nelson Carver — Ray Austin — Wesley Witham

Standish High School Basketball 1936
Winner - Gorham Normal Tournament

Standish High School played its first (recorded), boys interscholastic basketball game against Potter Academy of Sebago. The score was Potter 17, Standish 14.

March 16, 1789

A warrant for a town meeting was issued that contained, among other things, "To see what methods the town will take respecting a Pot. Ash for the use of the town."

Ashes from hardwood trees could then be used to make lye, which could be used to make soap or fertilizer. Apparently, a boat would visit locations on the lake to pick up ash.

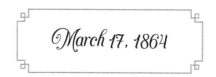

March 17, 1864

TO ALVAH WEEKS, CONSTABLE OF THE TOWN OF STANDISH IN THE COUNTY OF CUMBERLAND

Greetings:

In the name of the State of Maine, you are hereby required to notify and warn the inhabitants of said town of Standish qualified by those who vote in town affairs to assemble at the Town House in said town on Thursday the seventeenth day of March at two o'clock in the afternoon to act on the following articles:

1. To choose a moderator to preside in said meeting.

2. To determine what measures if any the town will adopt to pay the loan of three thousand dollars made under the vote taken at the meeting holden on the 24th day of February, 1864 two raise or appropriate any money that may be necessary to pay the said loan.

3. To determine whether the town will raise any money for the purpose of paying recruiting agents and other expenses of enlistment.

4. To determine whether the town will procure any more recruits for the service of the United States prior to another call for troops, and, if so, whether it will appropriate any part of the town obtained under the vote passed at the meeting holden on the 24th day of February 1864 for the purpose of paying such recruits.

—Joseph S. Tompson, Samuel O. Paine, Amos Boulter, Selectmen of Standish (the loan of February 1864 was to fund the bounty for recruits)

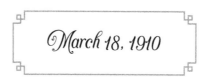

March 18, 1910

TO BUILD BIG DAM

Thousands of horse power to be developed at Bonny Eagle in Saco

Biddeford Maine, March 17—Extensive indeed is the undertaking which it would seem is mapped out for the next several years in the development of the water power along the Saco River, and there is enough of the detail already in process of materialization to give the public a fine idea of the extent of the enterprise. The plans already mapped out will take several years to accomplish and at Bonny Eagle and East Limington, the immediate field of operations, there is certain to be a lively lease of life.

Portland capitalists make up the company which has this project under way. It is the same company which recently installed the great electrical plant at West Buxton. Control has been secured of the water privilege at Bonny Eagle and a very large power plant at this point on Saco River is one of the improvements. The company is now furnishing electrical power to Portland and Sanford. The high-tension wire to Sanford has been but recently installed and it now supplies power to the Sanford Mills. As will be clearly seen, the details of the project contemplates one of the most expensive undertakings and the consummation of the different details will be watched with interest.

The plant which is to be constructed at Bonny Eagle, will make the one at Buxton seem small by comparison and it will develop thousands of horsepower. At this point, on the river, there is already a fall of many feet. This is to be increased by a dam of 80 feet in height and extending from one side of the gorge to the other. Its construction will require thousands of yards of material and the expenditure of a large sum of money.

The raising of this great dam will create a small lake at its back and this will extend to East Limington, a distance of five or six miles, with a width of over a mile in places. Already hundreds of acres of rich farm and forest lands which are to be flooded by this process, have either been purchased outright or bonded by the company.

One of the finest of these farms is in the A.C. Usher place, which contains nearly 150 acres and for what Mr. Usher is to receive $100 per acre. The owner of this place, as well as the proprietors of all other

Bonny Eagle, Me.

properties purchased, has been given the privilege of stripping the land of all growth and is allowed five years in which to complete this process. Furthermore, these property owners are to occupy their homes until driven out by the rising water. It is believed that the preliminary work for this plant will commence during the summer and pushed to completion as rapidly as possible, as however it is an immense undertaking, the property owners will not have to leave for some years to come.

During the prosecution of this work it will be necessary given the flow of the Saco River to construct a huge coffer dam. After the construction of this coffer dam, the right wing will be extended to cut off the flow of the Saco and force the water into the New River. From this point, it flows to the left for some distance, then parallels the Saco for some hundreds of yards after which it reenters the parent stream. This branch as it is at present is a raging torrent during every freshet.

The alterations which are going on at present in Limington while not nearly so extensive are nevertheless of great importance. Chase and Hubbard's Mills are located in this area which with their water privileges have been bonded by the promoters of this scheme for $20,000 each.

Lewiston Evening Journal

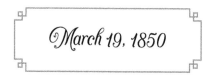

March 19, 1850

THE INDENTURE OF TING SMITH WITH JOSEPH SANBORN

This indenture made this nineteenth day of March 1850 by and between **Tyng Smith** of Standish in the County of Cumberland and State of Maine yeoman, and **Joseph Sanborn** of said Standish witnesseth.

That said, Tyng Smith doth by these presents, hereby place, bind, and relinquish all claims to his son **Tyng Smith Jr.** to the said Joseph Sanborn to dwell and serve him from this day until he, the said

Tyng Smith Jr., shall arrive to the age of twenty one years, and during said time the said Tyng Jr. shall well and faithfully serve his master, and shall give and devote to him his whole time and labour, that he shall not use ardent spirits, or practice gaming or other unlawful sports, nor waste, injure, or destroy the property of his master, but conduct himself in a sober temperate, honest manner, and as a good and faithful son aught to do, during all the time aforesaid - And the said Joseph Sanborn, for himself, his executors and administrators, doth hereby covenant with the said Tyng Smith that he will faithfully and constantly provide him with good, suitable, and sufficient food, lodging, and clothing and all other things necessary in sickness and health, and will train him up in the habits of industry temperance and virtue and give him common school education, and will at the expiration of his time furnish him with two suits of wearing apparel, and pay to the said Tyng Smith Jr. the sum of fifty dollars when his time is out. The said Tyng Smith Jr. was born August 24th 1844.

In testimony whereof the said parties have hereunto set their hands and seals this 19th day of March 1850

Signed sealed and delivered in the presence of

Tyng Smith

Catherine R. Sanborn

Joseph Sanborn

Tyng Smith was five years-old at the time of his indenture. Eight years later, Tyng Smith was thirteen years old and was incarcerated at the Reform School.

March 20, 1936

The covered bridge at Bonny Eagle was swept away in the historic flood of the Saco River and the ice floes carried down river.

The steel bridge between Standish and Limington was destroyed by the pressure of the high water and the force of ice floes.

March 22, 1841

TO THE OVERSEERS OF THE POOR OF STANDISH:

The undersigned, being a friend to mankind in general and more especially those whom fate, ill health or misfortune hath consigned to poverty and believing that such persons are not infrequently ill-treated and wrongfully dealt with by those who contract for their supplies and maintenance, wishes to be considered an applicant for the poor under your charge the ensuing year. The undersigned being possess'd of the conveniences necessary for such an undertaking fancies he could manage business of this kind in such a manner as would be satisfactory to all concerned. The undersigned would not wish to make a speculation of this, but wants a reasonable compensation for this trouble, and having considered the matter, believes that the sum of seven hundred and forty nine dollars to be as small a sum as he would propose, in order to clear the town from all further expense for the support of the poor the ensuing year.

Paul Knight

March 23, 1802

The Town of Standish issued a warrant for a town meeting to consider, among many other items, "to see if the town will allow the swine to run at large being yoked & rung according to law."

March 24, 1916

The last day Standish High School was housed in the Old Red Church.

Albion Parrish Howe was born at Standish.

Albion Parrish Howe was the son of Doctor **Ebenezer and Catherine Spring Howe**. *He was a graduate of the United States Military Academy, Class of 1841, and was an Assistant Professor of Mathematics there from 1843 to 1846. On October 1st, 1846, he was appointed Adjutant to the Fourth US Artillery. From there he served in the War with Mexico, the Expedition against the Sioux Indians, John Brown's raid, and during the Civil War. On March 13th, 1864 he was promoted to Brevetted Major General, US Army for "Gallant and Meritorious Service during the Rebellion."*

Moses Pearson, one of the founders of Pearsontown, was born in Newbury Massachusetts. He was a joiner (a house carpenter).

The first elections were held in the Town of Standish: **Theodore Mussey** was elected clerk; **Josiah Shaw**, Treasurer; selectmen were **Caleb Rowe**, **Daniel Mussey** & **John Deane**; Constable, **Sargent Shaw** and many others including such jobs as Thythingmen, Hogreaves, Informer of Deer and Sealer of Leather, Surveyors of Lumber and Cullers of Hoops and Staves.

To Mr. **Dominicus Mitchell** Treasurer of the town of Standish or his successors in office, you are hereby required to pay to **Isaac York** twelve shillings in full for his trouble and expense in taking care of the widow **Sarah York** in her sickness at his house.

John Deane, Daniel Hasty, Selectmen of Standish

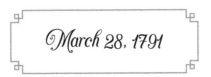

By vote of the town in town meeting on the 29th day of March AD 1829 - The Treasurer was directed to call upon the persons who had committed depredations upon the town magazine to restore the property taken and if such persons neglected to restore the same by the first day of May then next following to proceed according to law to obtain the same with damages -

In attending to the duties above assigned the following facts were ascertained:

- The lock by which the door of the magazine was supposed to be secured had for considerable time prior to the 1st of March 1830 been in such a situation that it was easily removed from the door without the aid of a key.

- The magazine had for several years been under the care of **Thomas Shaw** for which he had been paid by the selectmen or town.

- When the magazine was last inspected there were 350 pounds of Balls 400 hand - red flints.

- There was found in the magazine by the selectman after the depredations 173 pounds of balls & 302 flints showing a deficiency of 177 pounds of balls & 98 flints.

The persons against whom proof can be obtained of their taking away a part of this property are:

A son of Mr. Thomas Shaw about 18 years old - two boys of Mr. **Simeon Eaton** - two boys of Mr. **Isaac Davis** - two boys of Mr. **Jesse Butterfield**, two boys of Mr. **Wm Butterfield** all of which I believe are under fourteen years of age.

After obtaining all the proof that could be relied upon, your agent endeavored to effect a compromise with the parents of these boys and made an estimate of the value of the property missing & divided it into five equal parts & proposed to each individual to give a note for his proportion & then to lay the whole subject before the town for them to act upon as they might deem proper on condition that no one of these notes should be valid unless each & every other of the five persons before named should settle or pay his proportion - to this proposition four of the individuals being Mr. Shaw, Mr. Eaton & the two boys of Mr. Butterfield acceded. But Mr. Shaw, at a subsequent time, refused to give his note & informed me that he had a large account against the town that must come into settlement. Mr. Eaton, about this time, moved out of the place. Mr. Jesse Butterfield & Mr. Wm Butterfield gave, each, a note for five dollars which are now in the hands of the Treasurer.

Thus the only alternative left your Treasurer was to proceed criminally against these boys or prosecute Mr. Shaw for the whole amount of loss to the town - it was thought very doubtful whether the Treasurer wants to be justified in the first course & he did not feel authorized to prosecute half a dozen boys under fourteen years of age for theft without special direction of the town - & in the other case he thought it prudent to wait for the results of the settlement of Mr. Shaw's account with the town as this might be brought in to the same adjustment by the committee.

The Treasurer therefore asks to be excused from further duties upon this subject.

Respy Submitted - Oliver Frost Treasurer

March 30, 1789

The town issued a warrant to decide, among other things, "To see if the town will permit swine to run at large being yok'd and ring'd according to law" and "to see if the town will establish a road from the Meetinghouse to Saco River."

This road was to become Bonny Eagle Rd, Route 35. (Photo at right.)

March 31, 1828

Samuel Phinney purchased share no. 20 in the Capitol Stock of the Portland, Saco and Parsonsfield Stage Company.

Standish, Me., Looking S. W.

STANDISH, MAINE

EST

APRIL

1785

CUMBERLAND COUNTY

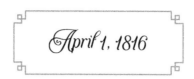

April 1, 1816

A STANDISH VOTING SCANDAL

Inasmuch as the subscribers have the most urgent reasons for supporting that in the choice of Messr. **Edmund Mussey Daniel Hasty Jr** & **John Spring** Selectmen elect - there was more votes assorted & counted than legal voters present in the meeting - they are therefore for the above reason protest against said choice. Standish April 1, 1816

For the Selectmen   92

others - - - - - - - -   82

Thomas Shaw
John Lowell
Samuel Dennett
Uriah Paine
Elliot Harmon
Tho's Paine Jr
Wm Butler
Joseph Paine Jnr
James ????
Daniel Moody
Green Cram
Edwd Tompson

April 2, 1911

Henry W. Swasey Esq., town attorney, billed the town for "advice on consultation as to liability of town for burial of a stranger killed on R. R. track and buried by order of Coroner holding inquest."

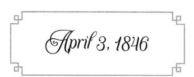

April 3, 1846

Amos Marean was paid $24.50 for building a school in District 13.

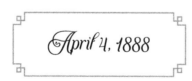

April 4, 1888

FROM THE STORE LEDGER OF LEMUEL RICH & SONS, SEBAGO LAKE

- C. I. Cole - 10 eggs 16¢

- **John DeCormier** - 2 quarts peas 16¢, vinegar 60¢, Tripe 14¢

- D. W. Stanley - Prunes 20¢, Starch 8¢

- Sawyer Clement - Butter 26¢, Corned Beef 23¢, Apricots 25¢

- **L. W. Moulton** - 2 lbs. coffee 50¢

- **Luther Blake** - 3 1/2 yards Dress goods $1.75

- Will. W. Stewart - 1 gal Molasses 44¢
- J. R. Hutchinson - 2 lbs. Lard 20¢, Oil 6¢, B. Sugar 14¢
- O. Ballard - Tripe 12¢, Tea 20¢, Sugar 16¢, Oil 10¢

- Ansel Higgins - Nails 9¢
- G. E. Whitney - Pork 35¢, Cheese 17¢
- Linnie Davis - Crackers 15¢

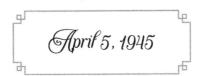

April 5, 1945

The Fire Department sponsored a free sound movie, a comedy, *Red Hot Rhythm* at Pythian Hall in Steep Falls.

April 6, 1931

The Town of Standish paid to the Student Council Body of Standish High School, **Manley Smith**, Treasurer, $50 as part payment for a Shower Bath. It was OK'd by Principal **Rupert Johnson**.

It was voted to build a new Meetinghouse at the expense of the town on parsonage land, the authorization for the construction of the Old Red Church.

The telephone lines at Watchic Lake, Dow's Corner and Standish Village were incorporated under the name "Standish Telephone Company."

Maquis G. Elwell, of Company K, 25th Maine infantry was killed in action at Pleasant Hill, the Battle of Red River, Louisiana. He was 20 years old and 17 days.

A newspaper described Pleasant Hill as "a little village situated on a low ridge, containing in peace-times probably 300 inhabitants." It further stated that, The battle-field of Pleasant Hill... is a large, open field, which had once been cultivated, but is now overgrown with weeds and bushes. The slightly-elevated centre of the field, from which the name Pleasant Hill is taken is nothing more than a long mound, hardly worthy of the name of hill. A semi-circular belt of timber runs around the field on the Shreveport side. At 5 p.m., the Confederate forces launched their attack, charging the entire Union line. The attack on the Union right had little success—the Union right, for the most part, held its ground. However, overall, this initial charge by the Confederates was highly successful and many of the positions down the Union left and center were overrun and the Union positions were forced backwards. However, the Union side succeeded in halting the advance and regained the left and center ground, before driving the Confederates from the field. The fiercely fought battle lasted about two hours. Losses were heavy on both sides, but the battle was considered a Confederate victory when the Union forces retreated.

—Wikipedia

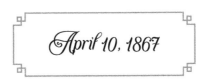

April 10, 1867

FROM THE DIARY OF JOHN P. MOULTON

Pleasant morning but soon commenced to cloud up and began to rain at 3:25 pm. In the fore noon, I burnt some brush in my pasture. In the afternoon, I trimmed up some apple trees. **Sarah** made soap.

I was up to father's just as night stopped a little while when I get home I found blacksmith **Martin** at our house, it is now 9:20 and her I guess would like to hear some go to bed and I am going.

April 11, 1957

The Portland Press Herald reported that **Rupert Johnson** ended his career.

Legendary coach Rupert Johnson coached both Baseball and Basketball. His baseball teams had an astounding record of 384 wins against 90 losses. They won 20 Triple C Championships, dominating high school baseball in this area.

Rupert Johnson
Standish High School Principal
Baseball & Basketball Coach

April 12, 1931

Mr. George E. Jack - Dear Sir:

I wish to tell you that I did not carry the scholars the last days of the last term on account of the condition of the roads. March 18th, 19th, 20th.

Very Truly, Mrs. **Harry True**

April 13, 1916

H. H. STURGIS WROTE TO THE BOARD OF ASSESSORS

"My real and personal property is the same as last year with the exception of automobiles, which consist of one Mitchell touring car Model 1913 and one Ford touring car Model 1915."

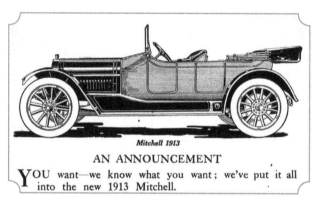

Mitchell 1913
AN ANNOUNCEMENT
YOU want—we know what you want; we've put it all into the new 1913 Mitchell.

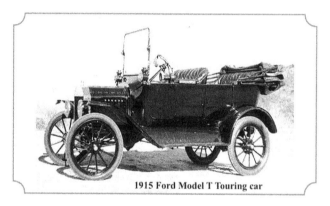

1915 Ford Model T Touring car

April 14, 1860

FROM THE DIARY OF JOHN P. MOULTON

Cold and windy, In the forenoon, I was fussing around, after noon we raised our barn. There was about 50 hands at the raising.

H. D. Ridlon, Steep Falls Bought of H. H. Hay's Sons (Wholesale & Retail Drugs & Chemicals, incorporated 1905 at the Junction of Free & Middle St in Portland) and shipped by Brown's Express 1 - 5000 Anti Toxin P. D. Co. for $7.50 less 10%, $6.75.

P. D. Company was Parke Davis, at that time the largest pharmaceutical company in the world. The Anti Toxin was a Diptheria Antitoxin developed in 1897.

"Voted that the meetinghouse which is to be erected should be situated upon the parsonage lot near **Daniel Hasty**'s in said Parish."

William Manchester Jr. wrote to his brother Nahum from Claremont Hospital in Alexandria VA:

".... I don't know as I can write you early news for you will hear by telegraph before this reaches you. President Lincoln was shot and died in about three hours. It is a great loss to this country as he was a noble man and a true patriot."

William was in Co. F 16th Maine Infantry.

April 18, 1855

The Fawn, the first passenger vessel to travel from Standish to Harrison, was sold by the Sebago and Long Pond Steam Navigation Company. Taking her maiden voyage in the summer of 1847, she had fallen on hard times as she competed with the Grand Trunk Railroad and Stage companies, all faster than a trip on the steamer. Stories of the Fawn's adventures on the water are told in "The Songo River Steamboats" by Holden & Knight, 1964 and "Sebago Lake Land" by **Herbert Jones**, 1949.

April 19, 1843

Dear Father and Mother,

We are sorry to learn (by your letter) that mother is so poorly, and Louisa thinks of coming over tomorrow or next day. We, at present, am all well - I was in Portland last week Grand Juryman and boarded at Leavitt's where Stephen lives - He is well and hearty - I bought up a bundle from him to go to Mother, cloth for shirts I believe, but when she will get it I can't say, unless Louisa goes over this week - I have to go to Salmon Falls once more and to Steep Falls twice more before my schools close - horrid traveling - I'm glad to hear that Lee is Rep. for Limington & Hollis and hope he will be selected in Sept. next. In haste, William Paine. P.S. We thank you for those Plougman's and shall want the rest of uncle Peter. - If Louisa should not come over, she will make Stephen's shirts if you can send the length of his collar in a letter.

(sent to **David Otis** *Esqr. P.M., Limington)*

April 20, 1750

The Massachusetts House of Representatives voted "that a township of the contents of six mile square on the northeast side of the line from Sebago Pond to Head of Berwick against Gorhamtown and No. 1 [Buxton] be and hereby is granted to Captain Humphrey Hobbs and Company and to Captain Moses Pearson and Company and to those who have signed the petition."

(Map on next page.)

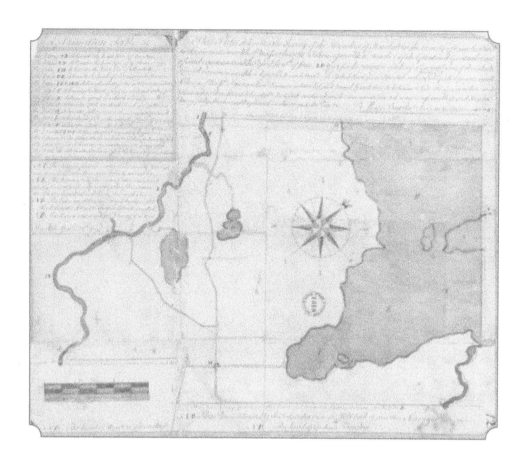

The Standish Municipal Center was dedicated.

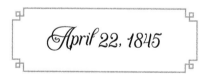

FROM THE GARDNER DENNETT STORE LEDGER

Marrett Thorn bought six bushels of ashes for $1.00, and **William Metcalf** bought 1 peck of Reese for 38¢.

There is no indication of what "reese" is. The ashes were used to make soap.

April 23, 1864

Jeremiah Hobson of Company I, 30th Maine Infantry was killed in action at the Battle of Cane River.

Although we don't have information relative to the entire action of the 30th Maine Infantry, to give a better understanding of when and where Jeremiah Hobson died, we do know this: [From Wikipedia] After being guided across the waist deep ford in the river, the Union soldiers slogged through a marsh before arriving at dry ground. They waded across a small bayou and marched about a mile before confronting a high hill defended by the Confederates. They were ordered to capture the position. A frontal assault was called with the 30th Maine Infantry in the center of the line. They advanced across an open field and up the hill. After taking the Union under brisk fire, the Confederates fell back and the Union occupied the hill. Jeremiah was 22 years old.

April 24, 1883

Boston - Selectmen: Town of Standish,

Will you please write me by return mail what action your town has taken about the road machine. I shall be home next week and, if you wish, will come to your town and operate the machine another day. If you will please give me an immediate answer, it will confer a favor as my time will be fully occupied in the eastern part of the state showing machines after the first of May. We have had orders for machines from almost every corner of Maine during the last month.

Yours Truly, **S. L. Adams**

April 25, 1893

Pursuant to a town warrant, the citizens of Standish voted "To see what action, if any, the town will take to locate the Free High School for which five hundred dollars was raised at the last annual meeting necessary to establish and maintain said school."

Standish High School opened that fall at the Old Red Church

April 26, 1958

Passenger service on the Maine Central's Mountain Division is discontinued.

April 27, 1871

To the Overseers of the Poor of the Town of Standish. Gentlemen:

You are hereby notified that **James H. Whitmere**, an inhabitant of your town, having fallen into distress, and in need of immediate relief in the town of Gorham, the same has been furnished by said town on the account and at the proper charge of the town of Standish, where said James Whitmere has legal settlement: you are requested to remove said James Whitmere or otherwise provide for him, without delay, and to defray the expense of support in said town of Gorham. The sums expended for support up, to this date are small... Said Whitmere fell from a team wagon, the wheels running over him and injuring him badly. Your town paid bills for Whitmere in the year 1868.

Yours with respect, Is **G. Bacon**, **Lewis Libby** Overseers of the Poor of Gorham.

April 28, 1795

Sir, Please to pay Mr. **Daniel How** seven shillings, the same being due him for flints for the use of the town and the same shall be allowed you on settlement.

Theodore Mussey, Treasurer
Peter Moulton, **Dominicus Mitchell**, Selectmen

April 29, 1868

Construction of the first conduit from Sebago Lake was started by the Portland Water Company.

Photo from 1920's construction

When two Bonny Eagle to see about **John Lane** who shot himself, wife and baby. Found him lying in the sitting room on the floor with a bullet hole in his forehead about two inches above the eyes in the center. The child was lying at his feet with a bullet hole in the left temple. His wife was lying on the floor in the dining room, lying on her left side with her arm under her head, in her night clothes with a bullet hole in the back of her head. It had passed through her head and came nearly through the head at the left temple and another in the back of the neck and lodged. It seems as if he had shot the child in the bed first, then his wife. So, he left the bed and he followed her to the dining room or else he carried her there. A hard struggle had taken place in the bedroom. He left a note on the table in the dining room, a deed and other papers, and a pocket book with three five-dollar bills. One bullet hole near top of the head on right side, one in back of head, and out left arm. "Bury me just as I am."

The writer is unknown and the note was found in the Standish Historical Society Archives. John W. Lane was 27 years old. He was the son of **Charles W. and Maria Anderson Lane**. *Mary, his wife was 28. She was the daughter of* **M. and Sarah Jane Fullerton**. *The baby,* **John Gordon Lane**, *was 10 days-old.*

STANDISH, MAINE
EST
MAY
1785
CUMBERLAND COUNTY

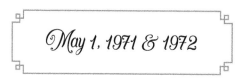

May 1, 1971 & 1972

The latest recorded Ice Out(s) on Sebago Lake in the 20th Century.

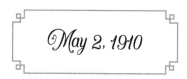

May 2, 1910

Steep Falls - **Arthur Warren** was dumping rubbish from a wheelbarrow into the Saco River when he lost his footing. After falling into the river and being carried over the dam, he managed cling to a rock in the river until he had rested and then swam to shore. It is a rather treacherous place in the river just above the dam and several who saw him go in expected to see him crushed to pieces as he went over the dam. His injuries summed up only a few scratches.

Portland Express-Advertiser

May 3, 1863

William H. Harmon of Company F, 7th Massachusetts Infantry, died at the Second Battle of Fredericksburg.

Major General John Sedgwick (Union) moved his forces into Fredericksburg during dawn on May 3, uniting with Brigadier General John Gibbon's division which had crossed the river just before dawn. Sedgwick originally planned to attack the ends of Marye's Heights, but a canal and a stream blocked the Union forces. He then decided to launch an attack on the Confederate center on the heights, which was manned by William Barksdale's brigade, with John Newton's division; this attack was defeated. Soldiers of the 7th Massachusetts caught a glimpse of the Confederate right flank and thought it looked unprotected. One of their officers requested a brief truce to gather in their wounded. Without consulting his brigade commander, Colonel Thomas M. Griffin of the 18th Mississippi Infantry granted it, allowing the Union soldiers to examine it more closely. Sedgwick launched another attack against this flank and Barksdale's front, using elements from all three VI Corps divisions, which pushed the Confederate forces off the ridge, capturing some artillery and the 18th and 21 Mississippi Regiments. The first men to mount the stone wall were from the 5th Wisconsin and the 6th Maine Infantry regiments. Barksdale retreated to Lee's Hill, where he attempted to make another stand but was again forced to retreat southward.

Wikipedia

William Harmon was 25 years old. He is buried in the Harding Cemetery.

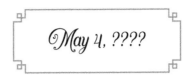

May 4, ????

Edward Tompson House Burned - The Old Landmark (located on the corner of Routes 25 & 35, where Websters Auto now stands)

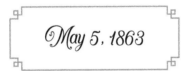

May 5, 1863

Charles E. Fogg, Company G, 17th ME, died as a result of wounds suffered at the Battle of Chancellorsville two days earlier on May 3rd.

The 17th Maine was in the thick of the fight on May 3rd at Chancellorville starting with a night attack where they lost one man. The losses to the regiment were much greater during the day as the regiment underwent one Confederate assault after another. The 17th Maine lost 113 of its 625 soldiers killed, wounded or missing. Their next campaign was Gettysburg.

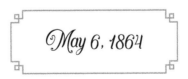

May 6, 1864

Charles A. Warren, Company H, 17th ME was wounded at the Battle of the Wilderness. He took a gunshot to the abdomen (bladder, rectum, hip, and backbone). He died March 1st, 1867 of his wounds. He left a widow and four children. He is buried in the Bonny Eagle cemetery.

At this time, the 17th ME was a part of the 2nd Brigade, 3rd Division, 2nd Army Corps under General Hancock. They engaged in fierce fighting throughout the day of May 6th about 20 miles from Fredricksburg, Virginia where they lost 24 killed, 147 wounded and 12 missing.

May 7, 1951

Ground was broken for the construction of the George E. Jack School.

May 8, 1888

The latest recorded Ice Out of Sebago Lake.

May 9, 1868

Pursuant to a warrant, the town met "To see what action the town will take in regard to building a stone pier under the Steep Falls Bridge or otherwise support said bridge...."

Rebuilding or repairing bridges and roads were a constant item at town meeting throughout the town's history.

May 10, 1819

At a legal meeting of the inhabitants of the town of Standish qualified to vote in town affairs on Monday the tenth of May 1819.

Art 1st Chose Col. **John Spring** Moderator

2nd Voted that the Selectmen shall Petition the Legislature of this Commonwealth for the separation of Maine from Massachusetts proper. Voted that **Nathan D. Appleton** and Major **James Hasty** be a committee added to the Selectmen for the above purpose.

Meeting dissolved.

Recorded by James Hasty Jr. Town Clerk

May 11, 1769

The first church, The Church of Christ, was established in Standish.

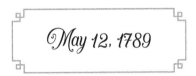

May 12, 1789

Pursuant to a town warrant for a town meeting, the voters met, "To see if said town will comply with the request of the committee of the town of Portland in respect to opening a passage from Sebago Pond into Little River in Gorham."

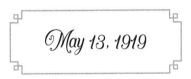

May 13, 1919

A patent was filed by **Joseph Boulet**, of Standish Maine for a Micrometer No. 1,303,245, Vol. 202, page 174 (Annual Report of the Commissioner of Patents for the Year 1919).

May 14, 1798

To the Honorable Members of the Legislature of the Commonwealth of Massachusetts in General Court assembled. The Petition of the inhabitants of the Town of Standish humbly Thewith? - that whereas said town had granted to them certain lots and parcels of land by the Proprietors thereof, for the use of their schools, and said lands being very little or no income and continually embezzlement's being made of the wood and timber of said lots which decreases their value. The town have therefore thought fit, and have sold at public auction the above said lands, on the following [ ] that the principal shall remain inter, and that the interest of the same shall be annually paid for the support of the schools.

We therefore request your honors to make legal said sale by your special resolve. And as in duty bond your petitioners will ever pray. **James D. Tucker, Dominicus Mitchell** - Committee to prefer a petition to the Legislature for the above purpose.

May 15, 1787

I, do truly and sincerely acknowledge, profess, testify, and declare, that the Commonwealth of Massachusetts is, and of right ought to be a free sovereign and independent State; and I do swear, that I will bear true faith and allegiance to the said Commonwealth, and that I will defend the same against traitorous conspiracies and all hostile attempts what-soever: and that I do renounce and abjure all allegiance, subjection and obedience to the King, of Great Britain, and every other foreign power whatsoever; And that no foreign Prince, person, Prelate, State or potentate, hath or ought to have any jurisdiction, superiority, pre-eminence authority dissenting?? or other power, in any matter, civil, ecclesiastical or spiritual, within this Commonwealth; except Constituents in the Congress of the United States; And I do further testify and declare, that no man or body of men hath or can have any right to ab??? or discharge

one from the obligation of this oath, declaration; and that I do make this acknowledgment, profession, testimony, declaration, denial renunciation, and abjuration, heartily and truly according to the common meaning and acceptation of the foregoing words, without any equivocation, mental evasion, or secret reservation whatsoever.

This may Certify that on the fifteenth Day of May AD 1787 **Theodore Mussey** Clerk of the Town of Standish took and subjected the Oath of allegiance as prescribed in the Constitution of the Commonwealth of Massachusetts

Before me, **John Dean** Just. peace

Theodore Mussey, Josiah Shaw, Jonathan Philbrick, Isaac S. Thompson, Peter Moulton, Enoch Linnel, Geo. Freeman, Dominicus Mitchell, Israel Thomes, Daniel Lowell, Thomas Shaw

The Congregational Church in Standish burned down. It was built in 1834. The fire started the day before, caused by a lightning strike.

John Monroe Graffam, 75, was robbed of $1000 in his hometown of Lynn MA just before embarking on a trip to Standish. He was a brother of **Emma Graffam Shaw**, of Sebago Lake, wife of **Perley Shaw**. He was jostled and pickpocketed shortly after receiving his money.

John Munroe Graffam
1857-1939

The Standish High School baseball team lost to the Bridgton Academy JV squad 10-9 at Bridgton, despite having beaten them 2-1 earlier in the season. This was the team's one loss of the season. They finished 14-1 defeating Gorham for the Inland Championship of the Triple C Conference and beat Cape Elizabeth twice, 4-1 and 5-1 for the overall Triple C Title. Batting averages were impressive:

- William Brazier .548,

- Roland Lewis .421,

- Norman Lindquist .375,

- Willard Austin .333,

- Raymond Lombard .333,

- Carl Bodge .314,

- Laurel Burnham .307,

- Stanley Austin .245,

- Raymond Lewis .200 and

- Olin Ryall .196

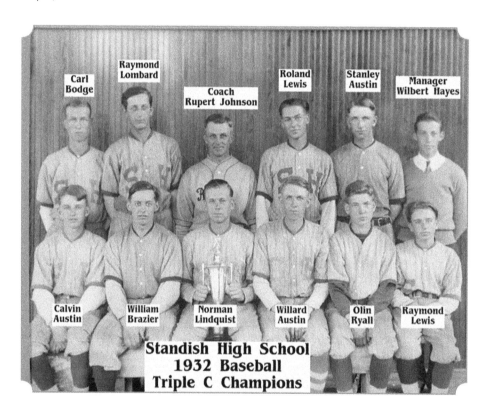

Standish High School
1932 Baseball
Triple C Champions

The Freewill Baptist Church at Steep Falls was incorporated with 25 members. The land was purchased from Tobias Lord which was, at the time, used as a lumber yard. A building committee provided their own funds and dedication was held in 1851.

Superior Court.

APRIL TERM—GODDARD, J., PRESIDING.

TUESDAY.—State vs. Thomas Parker, appellant. Search and seizure. Verdict, not guilty.

Webb.   O'Donnell.

State vs. John Drost, George Harmon and Leland S. Richardson. Indictment for assault and battery upon Savery, at Standish. On the fifth day of the term Drost pleaded not guilty. To-day he retracted his plea and pleaded guilty. It appearing that he had already suffered two months' imprisonment, he was sentenced to ten days imprisonment. Richardson was arraigned on the same indictment and pleaded *nolo contendere*. He was fined $5 and one third the costs of this Court.

Webb.   Swasey & Son.

Portland Daily Press - Assault

The Rupert Johnson Ballfield was dedicated. **Rupert Johnson** was the Standish High School (1924-1961) Principal, teacher, legendary baseball coach, basketball coach, bat maker, and first athletic director of Bonny Eagle High School.

Speakers included Town Manager **Scott Cole**, **Morton Strom** '50, **Wesley Dolloff** .41 and **Jean Cobb** '61.

Wesley Dolloff speaking at the dedication of Johnson Field

May 22, 1911

TWO STANDISH LADS GO WADING AND BOTH ARE DROWNED

The warm wave yesterday was responsible in part for the death of two Standish boys, who late in the afternoon removed their shoes and stockings and waded into Jose's brook. They walked into a deep hole and were drowned. The victims were **James B.**, 13, son of **Franklin Norton** and **Walter E.**, 11, the son of **Edgar Norton**. The waters are cousins and the latter is proprietor of a local hotel. **Carl Boulter**, aged 8, was the only witness of the accident. He screamed lustily for help and within two three minutes assistance was at hand, but the bodies were not recovered for an hour.

Kennebec Journal

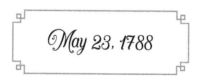

May 23, 1788

Please to pay to Mr. **Dominicus Mitchell** three pounds, three shillings that sum being due to him as allowed by the town, it being ten pence per pound for collecting thirty five pounds 3/6 (3 shillings, 6 pence) as a school tax and twenty six pounds 9/1 as a ministry tax and a county tax of fourteen pounds 6/8 1/4, the whole being 75...18...3 1/4 @ 10 pence per £ (75 pounds, 18 shillings, 3 pence, 1 farthing) - - The wages of the tax collector.

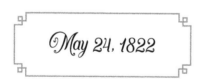

May 24, 1822

Bo't of Samuel Irish - A loom, quill wheel, spools 2c - $6.00. This day made delivery of the foregoing articles to Mr. Phinney & received payment in full therefor - **Samuel Irish**.

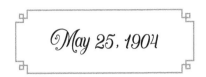

FROM THE AUTOGRAPH BOOK OF BESSIE HIGGINS

First but not foremost,

Your friend and Schoolmate **Grace E. Graffam**, Steep Falls.

Bessie Higgins '04

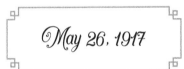

May 26, 1917

A bill from **L. O. Buzzell**, M.D. for services as Sec. Board of Health in including: Fumigating the Schoolhouse; Injecting Antitoxin, Taking Smears & Throat cultures and fumigating several residences.

(This was during the Influenza epidemic.)

May 27, 2002

The Standish Municipal Center WWII Memorial was dedicated.

May 28, 1787

A town warrant was issued to meet "To see what method said town will take to build a school house or houses." (it was still on the agenda six months later), A Town Warrant was issued to decide at a meeting on June 5th, among other things, **"To see if the said town will reconsider a vote that was passed at the last annual meeting that one person should not buy but one pew."**

May 29, 1788

A town order was issued to pay **Dominicus Mitchell** eighteen shillings, that being the sum due to him from the town for conveying a woman & children out of this town to Gorham and was allowed him at the annual meeting.

PHYSICIAN'S STAND AND BUSINESS, FOR SALE.

THE residence of the late Dr. Wm. B. Cobb, at Standish village, and the good will of his business are offered for sale on favorable terms. The premises are beautifully located and include a fine orchard. The situation presents great attraction for a good physician. For particulars address. MRS. ABBY H. COBB, Standish Me.
my13   d1m

Portland Daily Press - The Buzzell house

FROM GEORGE L. BROWNELL MANUFACTURER OF FINE HEARSES TO ALMON H. CRESSEY, SELECTMAN:

In reply to yours of the 26th, will say that I send you by mail photos of two of my popular styles of light fine Hearses. Am extensively engaged in their manufacture, building over 30 different patterns, ranging in price from $400 to $1500. They are all of best material & workmanship, of most modern styles, with latest improvements, and I warrant all my work. Please examine my list of Hearse Patrons and see the large number from your State - The Town of Gorham having purchased 3 of me. ... **George L. Brownell**

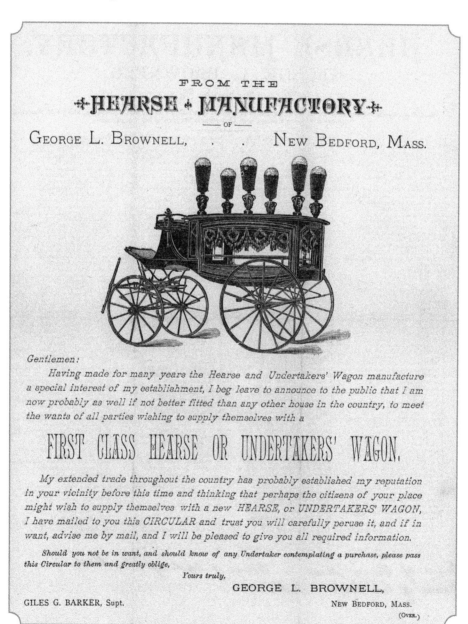

FROM THE

✦HEARSE ✦ MANUFACTORY✦

— OF —

GEORGE L. BROWNELL, . . NEW BEDFORD, MASS.

Gentlemen:

Having made for many years the Hearse and Undertakers' Wagon manufacture a special interest of my establishment, I beg leave to announce to the public that I am now probably as well if not better fitted than any other house in the country, to meet the wants of all parties wishing to supply themselves with a

FIRST CLASS HEARSE OR UNDERTAKERS' WAGON.

My extended trade throughout the country has probably established my reputation in your vicinity before this time and thinking that perhaps the citizens of your place might wish to supply themselves with a new HEARSE, or UNDERTAKERS' WAGON, I have mailed to you this CIRCULAR and trust you will carefully peruse it, and if in want, advise me by mail, and I will be pleased to give you all required information.

Should you not be in want, and should know of any Undertaker contemplating a purchase, please pass this Circular to them and greatly oblige,

Yours truly,

GEORGE L. BROWNELL,

NEW BEDFORD, MASS.

GILES G. BARKER, Supt.

(OVER.)

· STANDISH, MAINE ·

EST

JUNE

1785

CUMBERLAND COUNTY

June 1, 1830

The Cumberland & Oxford Canal opened.

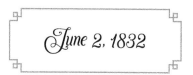

June 2, 1832

To the inhabitants of Standish in Town Meeting assembled June 4, 1832. **Nathaniel Whitney** of said town respectfully offers the following facts for the consideration of the town - First that he has been compelled to pay license as an Innholder when the greater part of his custom has been the accommodation of travelers to eat their own food. Second, that his wife has been unable to walk for four years & otherwise out of health - & that his age and feeble health has rendered him unable torn his living - whereby he has for several years been compelled to hire all done in & out for their support - and in addition to the trials thus named, his sons dependence for help has been complained about - months by a wound on the leg - all these added to physicians and nurse bills have become unsupportable by any man of his age & infirmities - have compelled him total down his sign and wholly abandon his Tavern - he further states that for allowing travelers treat at his table & selling occasionally a mess of oats & baiting of hay he has been compelled to renew his license or contend in law, while all facts of spirits have been denied tool travelers. He expects like all others today & has uniformly paid his full proportion of public taxes - But he considers it wrong that a public house kept former accommodation of teams with their own food and so retiree? as his should be liable for the same amount of license as those in the most public and profitable stand - for the above & many more reasons which may in truth be given he respectfully solicits of the town the abatement of the sum of $6.25 the amount of his license the current year. Which sum, though small for the town would be a great relief to him under present circumstances - and for which they will receive this sincere thanks.

June 3, 1884

The Presumpscot Water Power Company, as a result of their dam overflowing and causing damage to Littlefield Rd, paid the Town of Standish $2000 and promised to repair the road.

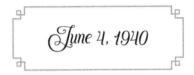

June 4, 1940

The Portland Press Herald reported the death of World War I veteran, **Lewis J. Hogan**. He received the French Croix de Guerre for gallantry under machine gun and artillery fire. He served in Company C of the 5th Machine Gun Battalion. He lived in Richville with his sister, **Annie Cole Hogan**. He never recovered from the effects of being gassed in the trenches, "mustard gas" being the most common chemical used during that war.

L to R, Dot Cole, Lewis Hogan, William Cole, Unknown, Annie Hogan Cole, John Hogan

Articles of agreement between **Jacob Berry** of Conway in the State of New Hampshire of the one part and the Inhabitants of the town of Standish in the County of Cumberland and State of Maine of the other part, as follows -

Whereas the abutment on the Standish side of the bridge over Saco River at Bonny Eagle, so called, has become ruinous, rendering the said bridge unsafe, and subjecting the said inhabitants to the necessity of repairing or in some way altering it, so that the same may be safe and convenient for the public travel.

And whereas the said Berry has proposed to the said inhabitants that the most advisable manner of repairing and fixing said bridge is to lengthen the Standish ends thereof about sixteen feet, by building an addition there to of that length so that the said end of the bridge may be made to rest upon a permanent foundation upon the ledge of rock there situate, and has proposed and offered to said inhabitants that he, the said Berry, in consideration of two hundred and fifty five dollars to be paid to him by said inhabitants as hereinafter stated will at his own proper expense and charge furnish all the lumber and materials of every kind required to repair and lengthen the said bridge as aforesaid and for securing the same preparatory to putting on said addition, that he will so secure said bridge preparatory to building the said addition, that he will erect and build the staid addition to the length of said bridge and in every proper way completely finish and secure the same and do and perform all things necessary and proper to be done in order to render the said bridge safe and convenient for the public travel, excepting the stone work, which the said inhabitants are to do -

and the said Berry agrees to warrant to said inhabitants the safety and uninjured condition of said bridge by said method of repairing it and that the same shall be and remain in every respect safe and convenient for the public travel. ...

June 6, 1999

Standish Voters approved a new Town Hall and Public Safety building. The vote was 739 to 636. It was built on 11 acres across from the former Hanold Clothing Factory on Route 35.

June 7, 1931

Standish High School won the Triple C Baseball Championship by beating Cape Elizabeth 2-1. The game was settled with a Triple play, where Norman Lindquist in right field picked up a grounder, threw to Raymond Cleaves on 2nd base for the first out, who relayed the ball to Willard Austin on first base for the 2nd out who threw to James Rand to prevent a Cape runner trying to score from second base. This capped a 16-2 season. Needless to say the batting averages were amazing:

– Raymond Cleaves	.523
– Walter Libby	.452
– Willard Austin	.416
– Stewart Hooper	.416
– Norman Lindquist	.368
– Carl Bodge	.365
– Roland Lewis	.341
– Roland Warren	.333
– Edward Whittier	.294
– Gerald Harmon	.278
– James Rand	.268
– LeRoy Lombard	.227
– Stanley Austin	.200
– Olin Ryall	.000

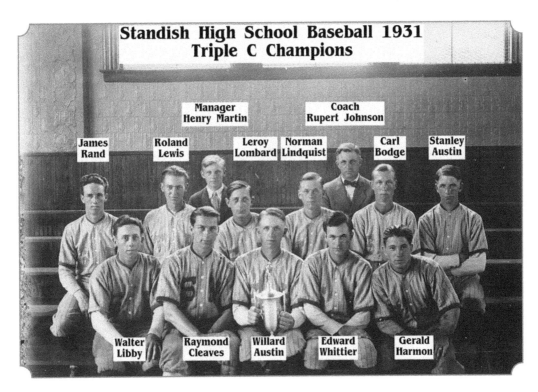

Standish High School Baseball 1931 Triple C Champions

June 8, 1847

FROM GARDNER DENNETT'S ACCOUNT LEDGER

Reuben Lowell purchased 1 pint of C. Brandy @35¢ and 1 1/2 pint of H. Gin @21¢ for medicine.

Referring back to January 18, the law has changed as all alcohol purchases are now for medicinal purposes.

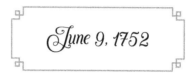

June 9, 1752

At a meeting of the grantees of a tract of land granted to Capt'n **Moses Pearson** and Company and Capt'n **Humphrey Hobbs** and Company joining Sebago pond, Gorhamtown No. 1 and Saco River - Voted that there be thirty three thirty acre lots in the middle of the town Reserved as followeth, one for the Ministry, one for the first settled minister and one for the School, the other thirty acre lots to be dragged for by the first third proprietors that shall appear and give bond for the fulfilling the condition of the settlement between this date and April next...

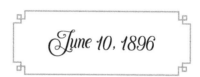

June 10, 1896

Rich's Mill burned to the ground in Richville.

Standish, Friend Moulton (**Willard Moulton,** Selectman) I have bin thinking about the fence and as some of my neighbors are fussy about what I do I guess we had better have a La... full fence and have it on the line. That will put a stop to the trouble. So, when you selectmen will come and run the line between me and the road I will put my fence on it. **G. M. Brown**

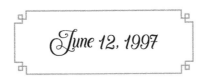

Governor **Angus King** signed into law an act to allow Frye's Island to secede from the Town of Standish.

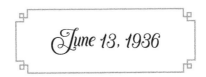

The A. F. Sanborn & Son Company building was destroyed by fire. The cause of the fire was presumed to be a tramp who had around the building.

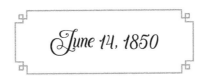

The selectmen of Standish authorized payment to **Reuben Lowell** one dollar and 75 cents for "Keeping a Strange Woman."

Standish School Board - voted that the action of the Principal of Standish High School, in suspending **Mildred Cressey** for leaving school during a session without his permission, be sustained, and that the suspension remain in force during the rest of the term unless she makes sufficient apology to the Principal and the school.

Mildred Cressey is not among the list of Standish High School graduates. It may be assumed that she did not return after this suspension. Mildred Louise Cressey, 17, in the 1910 Standish census was living at home with her parents, **Edwin & Nettie Marean Cressey.** *In 1913 she married* **George Brazier** *and lived in Sebago Lake Village.*

June 16, 1900

Between thirty and forty citizens from every section of the town gathered at the Town Hall, at Standish Village, to decide upon the advisability of taking some action toward welcoming the returning sons and daughters of Standish, during Old Home Week. The Maine Central Railroad gave the use of their extensive grounds at Sebago Lake Station and half fares from Portland to North Conway with four trains daily ... and thus started the planning and scheduling of events for the August 9th celebration.

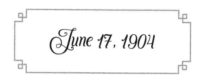

June 17, 1904

The First Banquet of the Standish High School Alumni Association was held.

The menu contained: Strawberries - Cold Boiled Ham, Cold Tongue with pickles and hot rolls - Lobster salad, Salad a la Alumni with Butter Thins, Saltines and Olives - Harlequin Ice Cream with Angel Food and Assorted Cake - Hot Chocolate with Whipped Cream and Coffee.

Toasts were given by **Edwin A. Moore** (Toastmaster), Address of Welcome, Response for Alumni by **Joseph T. Swasey**, Response for the Class of 1904 by **Frank E. Sawyer**, A Poem by **Edith A. Usher**, Standish High School - Its Past by **Mary J. Rand**, Our Boys by **Harriet M. Jordan**, Our Girls by **Edgar F. Weeman**, The Old Brown Church by **Ethel L. Higgins**, Oration by **Millard G. Boulter**, Athletics by **Leon G. Paine**, Our Teachers by **Royal C. Boulter**, and Standish High School Its Present by Principal **E. P. Goodwin**.

June 18, 1872

Gorham.

Gorham won three victories at base ball on Saturday. The Seminary Nine beat the Scouts of Standish by a score of 45 to 3; and then the Sebascoms used up the Rough and Readys of Saccarappa and the Regulators of Boston; the first by a score of 24 to 3, and the second 29 to 11.

Portland Daily Press

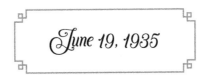

June 19, 1935

"To **Perley Fogg**: I have telephoned **Fred Cole** and he says to give this man his breakfast" **M. P. Boulter**. "Give this fellow supper, breakfast, and a place to stay" Fred Cole.

These vouchers were necessary for tramps to secure food and lodging at the Town Farm. Perley Fogg and his wife ran the Town Farm in 1935.

June 20, 1856

Dear Mother,

I expect by this time you are tired of L. and I am sure I am tired doing without her. I feel very anxious to hear from her for I am afraid she is sick, or discontented. But we shall know when Phoebe comes. We have concluded not to go after her 'till next week, (the muskets are so thick since the rain) if we can do without her, and she is well, but it seems to me a great while. I have felt very bad about the whooping-cough I knew they had it at Mr. Davis's but never thought of it till you had been gone sometime. Tell P. whether you went in or not. I hope you won't hunaon??? too much. I done not think about her I know P can't wait until next week. Do send all the particulars about her and if she is very homesick send her home with Phebe. Since writing the above, I have spent the afternoon alone, and I never was so lonesome. I shall go abroad tomorrow.

Yours with Love, Louisa

*(written to Mrs. **Anna S. Otis** of Limington, **John Otis** lived in Standish)*

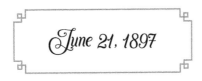

June 21, 1897

The first Graduation of Standish High school was held. The class motto was "Work has its own rewards." The class colors were Yellow and White. (Photo on next page.)

June 22, 1803

The Legislature of the Commonwealth of Massachusetts passed an Act to incorporate a number of inhabitants in the Town of Standish into a distinct religious society by the name of the First Baptist Society in Standish.

Standish High School 1896
Franklin B. Usher, Principal

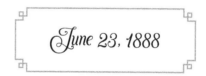

June 23, 1888

"Pursuant to a warrant from **Edwin C. Burleigh,** Treasurer of the State of Maine dated April 10, 1888, we have assessed the Polls and Estates of the inhabitants, and the Estates of the non-resident proprietors of the Town of Standish the sum of One Thousand seven hundred thirteen dollars 25 cents, and have committed lists thereof to the Collector of said Standish Viz: to **John E. Tompson** ... In witness whereof ... **Parker F. Paine, W. M. Libby,** assessors

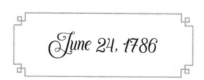

June 24, 1786

Commonwealth of Massachusetts, Senate: Whereas it appears to this court that the Resolve of the eighth of March 1786 abating a part of the taxes on the Town of Standish did not comets the knowledge of the said town till after the 15th of April the time limited therein for the assessors to be sworn: & that the assessors were sworn the third day after receiving said resolve.

Resolved that the town of Standish be & they are hereby declared to be entitled to all the benefit expressed in said resolve of the eighth of March last, the time limited by said resolve for the assessors to be sworn having elapsed before they were not sworn in withstanding

Sent down for concurrence, **Samuel Phillips Junior** President In the House of Representatives, June 24, 1786.

Read and concurred; **Artemus Ward,** Speaker: Approved - **James Bowdoin** (refer to March 8)

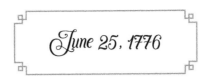

June 25, 1776

The Proprietors voted "that the Meetinghouse in Pearsontown be granted to the inhabitants of said Town for a house of Public Worship.

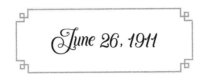

June 26, 1911

John Thompkins has had his house piped for water from the Benjamin E. Cousins fountain which supply a large number of families in the place.

Portland Press Herald - Steep Falls News

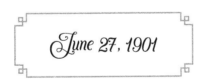

June 27, 1901

FROM THE DIARY OF GILBERT MOULTON OF SEBAGO LAKE VILLAGE

Very hot was in the (gravel) pit all day. I never worked there a hotter day. The thermometer registered 105° in the shade at home in the evening.

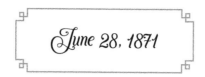

June 28, 1871

The Portland & Ogdensburg railroad's first accident occurred. An empty passenger train which had left Portland to bring back a party of Westbrook school children at Sebago Lake smashed into a loaded flatcar of stone in a work train backing around a curve to Sebago Lake and Otter Pond.

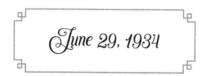

June 29, 1934

FROM THE DIARY OF GILBERT MOULTON OF SEBAGO LAKE VILLAGE

Very hot, at home all day. Put arsenic of lead on my potatoes. Today the bugs was awful thick. The weather bureau said it was the hottest June day that ever was recorded.

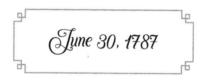

June 30, 1787

CUMBERLAND SS TO DOMINICUS MITCHELL, CONSTABLE OF THE TOWN OF STANDISH WITHIN THE COUNTY OF CUMBERLAND

Greeting

In the Name of the Common Wealth of Massachusetts you are required to levy and Collect of the Several persons Named in the lists herewith committed unto you it being their Proportion of a Tax of twenty three pound Eight shillings for the Support of the Gospel and thirty pound for the use of a School Voted at Legal Town Meeting on the twenty Sixth Day of March and Continued by adjournment to Monday, the Second day of April 1787 and you are to transmit and pay in the aforesaid Tax unto Deacon Jonathan Philbrick Town Treasurer or his Successor in office and to Compleat and make up your accounts by the first day of March Next — And if ant person shall refuse or neglect to pay the sum he is assessed in the said list to distrain the goods or chattles of Such person to the Value thereof. And the Distress so taken to keep for the Space of four days, at the Cost and Charge of the owner and if he shall not pay the sum so assessed within the Said four days, then you are to sell at public Venue the distress so taken for the payment thereof with Charges first giving forty eight hours. Notice of Such Sale by Posting up Advertisements in some public place in the town aforesaid and the overplus arising by Such Sail if any there be, besides the Sum aforesaid and the Necessary charges of taking and keeping the Distress you are immediately to return to the owner and for want of Goods or Chattles whereon to make Distress besides tools or implements necessary for his trade or occupation; Beats of the plough necessary for the Cultivation of his improved Land: Arms Utensils for Housekeeping necessary for upholding life bedding and apparel necessary for himself and family for the Space of twelve days you are to take the Body of Such person refusing or Neglecting And him Commit unto the Common Gaol of the County there to remain until he pay the Same or Such part thereof as Shall

— 108 —

not be abated by the Assessors for the time being; or the Court of the General Sessions of the peace for the said County

Given under our Hands and Seal at Standish this Thirtieth Day of June AD 1787

Josiah Shaw

Peter Moulton Assessors

Enoch Linnel

STANDISH, MAINE

EST

JULY

1785

CUMBERLAND COUNTY

The new Steep Falls Bridge is opened replacing the bridge that was washed away in the flood in the spring of 1936. The first bridge over the Saco River was built in 1859. It was a covered bridge.

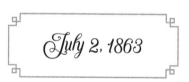

July 2, 1863

Robert B. Whitcomb of Company H, 17th Maine Infantry and **Charles M White** of Company I, 17th Maine Infantry were wounded at the Battle of Gettysburg. Whitcomb was wounded in the leg while White was wounded in the arm.

The information available on the 17th ME Infantry at Gettysburg is extensive and best read in its entirety. Suffice it to say that the 17th was involved in heavy fire and hand to hand combat, fighting to the point of no ammunition. They held their ground.

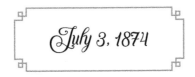

July 3, 1874

The Town of Standish filed a brief with the Supreme Judicial Court. Cumberland County in the case of The Portland and Ogdensburg Railroad vs the Inhabitants of the Town of Standish. The argument was that despite the vote of Standish to raise money to aid in the construction, $20,000, in exchange for 200 shares of stock there was no contract made between the town and the railroad, therefore the Railroad couldn't force Standish to pay. (Standish did not receive any stock).

July 4, 1833

"In consequence of difference of opinion in relation to religious affairs, existing among the members of the first Church and Parish in Standish, a large part of the former and many of the latter separated themselves from the said Church and Parish, and subscribed some more, and some less, for the purpose of erecting a new meetinghouse in this town for the use of said subscribers, and such others as may hereafter wish to associate with them."

(Book 1 Records of the Evangelical Congregational Society of Standish)

July 5, 1871

The pavilion at Sebago Lake opened. Chandler's Band provided dance music.

Park at Sebago Lake Maine

July 6, 1970

The Richville Library Burned. It is still located at the corner of Route 114 and Cole's Hill Road.

Richville Library

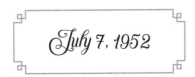

July 7, 1952

The **Pinkham** Quadruplets were born at the Osteopathic Hospital on Brighton Avenue in Portland. **Rebecca**, **Billy**, **Melissa** and **Jane** would be followed by the news throughout their childhood and young adult years.

July 8, 1822

To the Town Clerk of Standish

This is to give you information that on the 8th day of July 1822 § were found doing damage in the Field of **Sam'l Davenport** seven sheep Mark Crop off the right ear with two slits in the same, owned by **Stephen Cram** of Standish & I have impounded the same sheep in the Town Pound & within twenty four hours then next following gave him notice then of, in writing, & left with the Pound Keeper at the time they were committed a memorandum in writing, under my hand, of the cause of impounding & the sum I demand in damages from the owner before they are liberated - & although two full days have elapsed since the impounding, yet he has not paid the said damages & charges, nor has he replevied the same sheep - The amount of damages have been estimated by the men appointed by you at 3 Dolls. **Daniel Marrett Jr.** field Driver

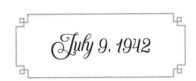

July 9, 1942

FROM THE DIARY OF GILBERT MOULTON

Clowdy and not as warm. At home all day and evening. We had some very hard showers this afternoon, it done lots of damage in Buxton. Hail and wind spoiled lots of their gardens. Went down to the Schoolhouse and registered for gasolene, a fool trick. Still raining tonight. 60° tonight.

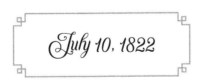

July 10, 1822

The above named **Daniel Marrett Jr.** personally appeared & made oath that the above information of the said transaction is correct & true - (see July 8th).

Before me **J. Hasty Jr.** Town Clerk

July 11, 1895

From the Rich & Son store ledger:

Sold -

- **A. Moody**, Boots $2.25, Pants $3.00;

- **George Whitney**, Hat $3.00;

- **Jarius Hanscom**, white lead .24; O. Ballard 3 spokes, .30;

- **O. Dole**, Sugar .50;

- **J. R. Hutchinson**, Cocoa .28;

- **William Harmon**, Flannel .48, Sitting .56, cash $5.00;

- **Delbert Libby**, Tobacco .10;

- **M. F. Longfellow**, salve .15, soap .10, tarts .09;

- **R. J. Shaw**, soap .50, pork .90, potatoes .80, r. oats .20, lard .30

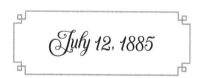

July 12, 1885

FROM THE AUTOGRAPH BOOK OF NELLIE A. SHAW

Let this little book go far and near,
To all of Nellie's friends so dear.
Let each entitle do her a page,
That she may read in her old age.
Your friend **Flora B. Evans**

Nellie A. Shaw *was born in 1872 making her 13 years old in 1885. In 1900, she would marry* **Herbert L. Rich** *and together they raised five children. She died in 1965 and is buried in Hamlin Cemetery.* **Flora B. Evans** *was born in 1871 making her about 14 years old here. In 1893, she would marry* **Mulbury Harmon Jr.** *and together they raised 10 children. She died in 1927 and is also buried in Hamlin Cemetery.*

July 13, 1801

To **Theodore Mussey** town treasurer please to pay Capt. **Joseph Dow** thirteen dollars & fifty cents it being due to him for his services as Selectman for the year 1800 and the same be allowed you on Settlement. **Peter Moulton, Daniel Hasty, Josiah Shaw**, Selectmen.

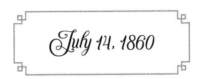

July 14, 1860

Windham, A complaint from **N. S. Kennard** about the Standish Roads.

Messes. Selectmen of the Town of Standish, this is told you that I had occasion to pass through your town from my place in Windham to Baldwin on the fourteenth day of last month and took the road leading from Hamlins to Steep Falls, as I had been accustomed to do both summer and winter, after leaving Hamlins we found a poor road until we arrived at the plains, there it appeared as though there had been one ox sled through some time in the course of the winter, In this part of the road the snow was very deep and very stiff it would about half bear the horse and she would plunge headlong almost every step and I expected we should some as be killed as the sleigh came well-nigh tiring over several times. We kept on a while in this way hoping to find the road better soon; but when we had got within one mile as near as we could judge of the west end of the road here we were stop entirely the snow had not been broken for the winter. There we were, in the middle of these woods in a cold winters day with no road and our horse tired and hungry and within same two or three miles of our journeys end. Now to go ahead was impossible. Here our horse appeared very much fatigued but there was only on way for us and that was to turn and make the best of our way out which was done with much fatigue to myself and horse; we called at J. Thompsons at Standish Corner and gave our horse some refreshment after which we performed the remainder of our journey and arrived at Col. N. Sawyers about 11 o clock; making our journey some 12 or 14 miles longer and out in the cold some three hours longer that we should have been if we had found a road as we had expected.

Now this is to request you to pay me 25 dollars just about what the horse was damaged or pay just what fine may be imposed on you for letting a county road lay till the 1st day of January and not be broke out.

Respectfully yours. N. S. Kennard, Windham Maine

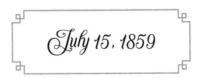

July 15, 1859

The State of Maine Treasury office notified the Treasurer of the Town of Standish that "The sum of $259.40 has been apportioned to the town of Standish as its proportion of the State School Funds distributed for the year 1859."

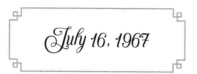

There was an explosion at the Sebago Lake Garage. Caused by a compressed air tank, it blew out windows and caused other damage. No one was injured as the blast occurred at 2:30am when no one was there. The garage is owned by **Herbert Woodbrey** who lives next door. The building stands at the corner of Routes 114 and 35.

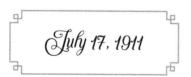

July 17, 1911

Hon. **Benjamin E. Cousins**, who has charge of the water supply in town [Steep Falls] has put water into the homes of **Charles Moore**, **Willard Hodgdon** and **Herbert Thomes** and he will soon put it in the station of the Maine Central Railroad and in the homes of **Stephen H. Cousins** and Mrs. **Emma L. Bailey**

Portland Press Herald

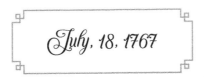

Daniel Marrett was born in Lexington Massachusetts.

July 19, 1876

The reform clubs of Sebago and White Rock held a very enthusiastic temperance meeting at Sebago Lake last Saturday evening. Between 200 and 300 of the reformers were present and they were jubilant over the fact that they can go through the busy season without intoxicating drinks. The reform movement in all that section is onward.

Portland Daily Press

July 20, 1906

FROM THE DIARY OF GILBERT MOULTON

Awful hot, was on the route until 3:50 PM, around house rest of day and evening. **Elmer Ford**'s and **Jarius Hanscom**'s houses was burned this afternoon also **Mulbry Harmon**'s and **Will Furlong**'s Houses. They think that Elmer's little boy set them afire. At home in the evening.

July 21, 1873

To **Bion Bradbury**, Esq. Portland,

Dear Sir, Yours of the 19th received saying the Sheriff shipped the two barrels of Rum to me per Maine Central the day previous. They are not yet to hand & I think there may be some irregularity somewhere. I enclose ten dollars / $10.

Very truly yours, **William Mann**

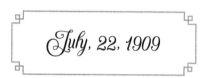

July, 22, 1909

Charles Moores's house [in Steep Falls] was struck by lightning last Saturday. The lightning came in at one corner of the house and went through every room and four panes of glass were broken. Miss **Mabel Moore** was the only member of the family who received any shock from it.

Portland Press Herald

July 23, 1942

FROM THE STANDISH HIGH SCHOOL AUTOGRAPH BOOK OF ARLENE CROWLEY (LEPON), CLASS OF 1942

Dear Arlene,

Just reminding you to remember "Ocean Anchor" and our first chocolate pie. Remember the night we met our good looking friend and also the cat. The squeek in the door was rather annoying (ahem) wasn't it. Heres' hoping our next four weeks go as fast as the first four.

Your "bed fella", **Mary Coolbroth**.

Arlene Crowley '42

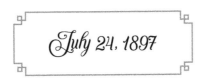

July 24, 1897

Selectmen of Standish,

I hear from a reliable source that you have been corresponding with a crasey lunatic of a woman by the name of **Ann Walker** of Wellington Maine.

Her mother died crasey and she is about the same. Next time you write her, you tell her I only pay my taxes in one town the same year.

Respectfully, **W. F. Chase**

July 25, 1937

FROM THE DIARY OF GILBERT MOULTON

Found tucked into July 25th, a ticket for the Irish Sweepstakes.

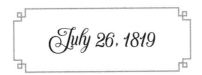

July 26, 1819

At a legal meeting of the Inhabitants of the Town of Standish in the County of Cumberland qualified to vote for Governor or Senators holden on the fourth Monday of July being the twenty sixth day of said month A.D. 1819 for the purpose of giving in their votes on this question "Is it expedient that the District of Maine shall become a Separate and Independent State, upon the terms and conditions provided in an Act, entitled An Act relating to the Separation of the District of Maine from Massachusetts proper, and forming the same into a Separate and independent State?"

The whole number of votes given in, in said town were sorted, counted, and declaration thereof made, and were two hundred and two of which one hundred and forty three were in favor of the Separation of said District from Massachusetts proper and for forming the same into a Separate and Independent State, agreeably to the provisions of said act; and fifty nine votes were against said Separation.

Recorded by **James Hasty Jr.** Town Clerk

July 27, 1917

Leander Dole sailed for Europe on the "Adriatic." He enlisted at Portland on June 12, 1917 and reported to Rockingham Park in Salem NH. He sailed for Europe July 27th, 1917. The 14th Engineers were the

first American troops on English soil and marched by Buckingham Palace parading before the King, Queen and others. On August 18, 1917, they were on the front in France. He became a cook during his service: "Dad did not enlist as a cook. One day, when they were in France, some of the fellows were taking a walk thru the fields and found two pumpkins. They brought them back to camp and my father made pumpkin pies. An officer happened to walk by as they were cooling, spotted the pies and confiscated one for the officer's mess. The rest, as they say is history." Leander A. Dole, Pvt. Co. C 14th Engineers discharged May 2, 1919

Information from **Mary E. Dole Jackson**

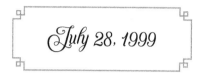

July 28, 1999

Dave Cousins won the Gold Medal in Men's Compound Bow at the World Archery championships and another gold in Team Compound Bow.

July 29, 1956

The ground was broken for the Center hospital.

July 30, 1898

John L. Chase was paid fifteen dollars for his sheep that were killed by dogs.

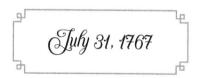

July 31, 1767

A violent hurricane commenced near Sebago Pond, took an easterly direction passing through the northeast corner of Gorham, crossed the Presumpscot at Lovett's Falls, passed through the middle of Windham, directly over Duck Pond, through the north part of Falmouth, and the south part of North Yarmouth to the sea. It extended the breath of three-fourths of a mile.

From History of the Town of Windham by Thomas Laurens Smith, 1873, published by Hoyt & Fogg, Portland, page 23.

August 1, 1974

The Standish Historical Society held their first meeting at the **Daniel Marrett** House.

Daniel Marrett House

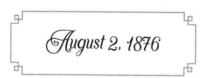

August 2, 1876

Steep Falls, **Henry M. Chadbourne** Esq. Chairman of the Selectmen of Town of Standish.

Dear Sir:

Thomas Skillings told me this morning that his wife has left him & that he is not able to do anything & that he would like for you to come up to see to his care at once. I really think Thomas is not well & under the circumstances you had better take him & his family on to the farm as his wife is no help to him & never will be unless she changes her course & tries to do better in the future than she has done in the past.

—S. H. Cousins

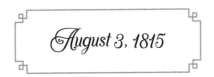

August 3, 1815

FROM LEVI SANBORN'S DAY BOOK

- **Thomas Paine Jr.,** 2 quarts Molasses .43, 1 pint rum, 6 eggs, tobacco, 1/2 pound coffee, 2 glasses rum. Rum by the gill .08
- **Israel Rich,** 1 silk 6/ $1.80
- **Enoch Marean,** credit by hauling 1 barrel rum & 1 barrel bread from Portland .67
- **James Beson** 1 quart molasses .26, 1 glass rum .04
- **Robard Higgins,** credit by your oxen and cart twice to Mr. Eatons .40

August 4, 1865

TO THE OVERSEERS OF THE POOR OF THE TOWN OF STANDISH IN THE COUNTY OF CUMBERLAND IN THE STATE OF MAINE

Gentlemen: You are hereby notified that **John A. Bragdon**, an inhabitant of your town, having fallen into distress, and in need of immediate relief, in the town of Westbrook, the same has been furnished by said town on the account and at proper charge of the town of Standish where said John A. Bragdon has his legal settlement; you are hereby requested to remove John A. Bragdon or otherwise provide for him without delay, and to defray the expense of his support unto this date. **Jonas Raymond**, Chairman, Overseers of the Poor of Westbrook. N. B. This boy is an idle youth and his father says he shall claim pay for his board from this date, and I think the boy is capable of doing enough to pay his board.

J. R.

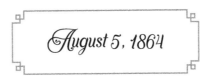

August 5, 1864

$350 for value received we the Subscribers Selectmen of Standish in Accordance with a vote of said town passed April fourth A. D. 1864 for the aid of families of volunteers promise to pay **Albert F. McDonald** on Order three hundred and fifty dollars in one year with interest. **Joseph S. Tompson, Samuel O. Paine:** Selectmen of Standish

Albert F. McDonald, Co. K, 25th Maine Infantry was born in Gorham in 1842. He was 20 when he enlisted in the Army, living in Standish at that time. At some point, he moved to Minneapolis, Minnesota where he married and later died. He was one of many in Standish who received support for their service in the Civil War.

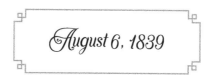

August 6, 1839

A bill from Captain **A. Berry** and Officers to **S. Phinney**. $3.34 for 1 quart each, Rum, Gin, Wine, Brandy, Gin and 6 pounds of sugar and a tip (to house) of $1.00.

Captain Berry and his officers, as the militia expected this to be covered as part of their expenses. Evidently this wasn't the first time and was, obviously, a bit controversial for the townsfolk.

August 7, 1949

FROM THE DIARY OF GILBERT MOULTON

Pleasant and hot. At home all day and evening. Chubby moved his store up here today and Harold and Edie have gone down there tonight. Traffic has been awful today - more than 300 cars an hour. 77 above tonight.

To the Selectmen of the Town of Standish:

We the undersigned legal voters in said town respectfully petition you to call a meeting of said town at your earliest convenience to see if the town will vote to exempt from taxation for a term of five years the mill property and manufacturing interests pertaining thereto of **Isaac L. Came** at Bonny Eagle on the condition that he rebuilds the dam and continues in the business of lumber manufacturing at that place.

Signed: **Orville S. Sanborn, William H. Sturgis, H. H. Sturgis, O. P. Warren, A. P. Berry, M. H. Sawyer, William M. Davis, John Haley, G. B. Pendexter, H. B. Hartford**

Nathan F. Whitney was killed in action at the Battle of Cedar Mountain in Virginia. He was a member of Co. E, 10th Maine Infantry.

The Battle of Cedar Mountain, also known as Slaughter Mountain, took place August 9th, 11862 in Culpepper County Virginia. The Union forces attacked General Stonewall Jackson's forces. A confederate counterattack resulted in a victory for Jackson. The name Slaughter Mountain is appropriate as the Union was outnumbered two to one and at a strategic disadvantage. The 10th Maine Infantry was ordered to hold off the Confederates long enough for the rest of the regiment to withdraw. The 461 man regiment lost 179 men in a fight that some survivors claim lasted as long as five minutes.

Wikipedia

The Saco River Electric Railroad accepted a permit from the selectmen of Standish for the location of its street railroad. It was to run from Saco near the Biddeford line, through Saco, Buxton, Bar Mills, West Buxton to Bonny Eagle a distance of 19 miles.

To the Selectmen, or the Municipal Officers of the Town of Standish, in the County of Cumberland, State of Maine:

The Saco River Electric Railroad respectfully petitions your honorable body for the right to lay single and double track or tracks with all necessary switches, curves, frogs and turnouts, together with entrances to car-houses, repair shops, power stations and stables, with spurs and switches upon and along public highways and roads in the Town of Standish; beginning at a point called Bonny Eagle in said town, and running to the line between Standish and Buxton over and along the Stage Road, so called, leading to West Buxton Village, in the town of Buxton in the County of York, in the State of Maine, to the end that persons, property and cars may be conveniently conveyed over said road.

With the right to erect all necessary poles equipped with brackets, wires and braces for the purpose of enabling your petitioners to operate said Saco River Electric Railroad by electricity, or compressed air, granting to your petitioners the right to occupy and use the whole or any part of said public highways and streets as your petitioners may elect, under such conditions and requirements as to posts or poles, kind thereof, height of and places where same may be set, height at which wires may be hung, as your honorable body may determine to be safe, as well as just and convenient to your petitioners.

Your petitioners further ask for such order of notice and hearing as the law requires and such written permits and approvals relative hereto as is provided by Law.

Dated at Biddeford, County of York in the State of Maine, this _twenty seventh_ day of July, A. D. 1897.

Charles S. Hamilton

DIRECTORS.

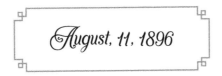

August, 11, 1896

FROM LULAH WADLEIGH'S DIARY

"Dr. Randall sold out to Dr. Buzzell." Later that month Dr. Buzzell moved his family here.

The house, although a house of many Doctors of Standish, is has been known as the Buzzell House. It was torn down in 2022.

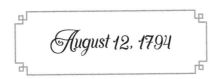

August 12, 1794

To **Theodore Mussey**, Clerk of the Town of Standish:

The following is the marks of a stray ox which broke into my enclosure on the 19th day of July last, Viz - a brindle color with a star on his forehead with some white under his belly, crop off his right ear & a Swallow's tail in the left.

Ebenezer Irish.

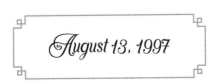

August 13, 1997

A hot air balloon descended on Bonny Eagle Pond. The balloon didn't land on the pond, but ascended quickly.

August 14, 1862

William Manchester Jr. enlisted as a private in Company F, 16th Maine Infantry at the age of 23. He was promoted to full corporal in 1863. He was wounded on May 8, 1864 at Laurel Hill, VA and discharged on May 22, 1865. The wound was a gunshot to the right hand. The battle was otherwise known as the Battle of Spotsylvania Court House - Laurel Hill

August 15, 1887

We the undersigned, residents of Sebago Lake Village, do hereby call your attention to the condition of a street in said village, running from the Pond Road (so called) to the Pleasure Grounds. Our interests, as property holders. on said street, as well as the public safety demand that the line of said street should be established, the obstructions removed, and its lawful width maintained, being, as it is the only thoroughfare to the Pleasure Grounds.

Signed: **Alpheus Davis, E. Higgins Parker, J. S. Webster, John Decormier, Orin Ballard, Eugene H. Parker.**

Today this "Street" is the part of Route 35, Chadbourne Road, running from the intersection of Routes 35 and 237, at the Portland Water District office to the intersection of Routes 35 and 114 in Sebago Lake village. The Pleasure Grounds would be the train Station, Pavilion and grounds located where the Boat Launch now stands.

August 16, 1944

FROM THE DIARY OF GILBERT MOULTON

Pleasant and awful hot, 100° in the shade. At home all day, after supper I took Bertha and drove to No. Windham and around to White's Bridge, watched the bathers and home by the back road. She seemed to enjoy it. We got home at 7:45. 78° tonight.

White's Bridge

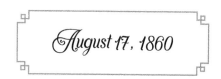

August 17, 1860

FROM THE DIARY OF JOHN P. MOULTON, SEBAGO LAKE

Warm and Pleasant - We got in two loads of oats and then Simon, Father and I went to Portland. **Stephen A. Douglass** was in there and I shook hands with him. He spoke twice there. Was between 10 & 15 thousand there.

Presidential candidate Douglass is pictured to the right.

August 18, 1847

The Steamboat, the Fawn, the first passenger steamer on the lake, made its maiden voyage. She wasn't a financial success because she was poorly balanced. In short turns she would tip causing one of the paddle wheels to lift out of the water. She was eventually dismantled and the engine and boilers were taken out and sold.

August, 19, 1909

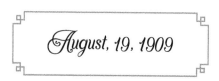

Hon. **Benjamin E. Cousins** and **Edwin R. Wingate** have purchased a bell which they will present to the town for the graded school building which is being built at this place. (Steep Falls)

Portland Evening Express

Steep Falls - Steep Falls was thrown almost into a panic today by a forest fire that threatened the destruction of the village. The flames, which formed a solid wall for fully three miles to the eastward of the village, gave every indication of spreading into the outskirts of the settlement. So frightened did the inhabitants become that telephone messages were sent to the Cornish fairgrounds 10 miles away for the Steep Falls residents who were attending the fair to hurry home and assist in fighting the flames.

Portland Daily Press

Bonny Eagle High School was dedicated and the old High School at Sebago Lake village was renamed Johnson Junior High School after Principal Rupert Johnson. It held grades 6 to 8.

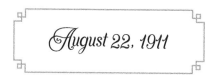

August 22, 1911

Twelve young French People from Waterville took the wrong train home from noon Station after their trip to Old Orchard Beach and came to Steep Falls. Four stayed overnight at Marean's Hotel. A collection was taken at the station to defray their expenses. The others hired **Woodbury Wadleigh** and **Ervin Bailey** to take them to Waterville Sunday night.

August 23, 1869

A bill was submitted by **William Jordan** to the Town of Standish for "damage done my carriage on highway near Standish Village on the Cornish road for $20. It was settled November 12 for $15.

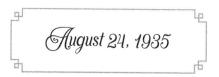

August 24, 1935

A Boulder was placed on the site of the Fort at Standish Corner during the Standish Sesquicentennial, the 150th anniversary of the incorporation of the town of Standish.

Below, (left to right) **H. A D. Hurd**, Mrs. **Harold Dolloff**, **Wesley Dolloff**, **Laura Dolloff**, Mrs. **Guy Sanborn** and Miss **Ethel Higgins** stand with the newly placed stone.

Standish Sesqui-Centennial
1935

H. A. D. Hurd   Wesley Dolloff

Mrs. Harold Dolloff   Laura Dolloff   Mrs. Guy Sanborn   Miss Ethel Higgins

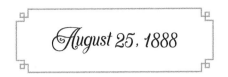
August 25, 1888

Dear Sir:

Your confidential letter to me dated August 17, 1888 came duly to hand: And in like confidence I write in answer to day to you that I infer from your letter that you may think **Isaac Dillingham** gained a pauper settlement in Buxton. And with a desire to save all useless expense, I now tell you that while Isaac Dillingham lived several years in the village off West Buxton - more familiarly called "Moderation" - that the village lays on both sides of the Saco river and in the towns of Buxton and Hollis, in both of which towns he lived meanwhile and neither of which did he gain a pauper settlement. If you desire some little time to satisfy yourself of the accuracy of this statement please so inform me and if you desire to make no further investigation of the matter be so kind as to let me know this as our Board must bring our claim to a speedy settlement.

Awaiting your early reply - (Name indistinguishable)

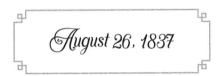
August 26, 1837

The undersigned, being a Committee chosen by the first parish in Standish on the seventeenth day of July last to confer with a Committee of Subscribers for an Academy, upon the plan of relinquishing the upper story of our Meeting-house to them. Report that we have agreed to and accepted the Proposals of the said Subscribers Committee upon the following conditions; viz. that said upper story be used for an Academy for literary and scientific purposes only: that the lower part of the House be finished in such manner as may be hereafter agreed upon by a committee: the Academy shall be free from Sectarianism, and when it ceases to operate the said upper story shall revert to the said first parish. Saturday August 26, 1837, **William Paine, Thomas Cram Jr., Daniel Poole**

Standish Academy opened its doors in 1847 and closed 10 years later, unable to meet recruitment goals and finding lodging for its scholars.

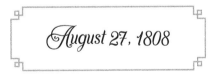
August 27, 1808

A Town meeting was held to "Take into consideration the expediency of Petitioning the President of the United States for a suspension of the several laws laying an embargo."

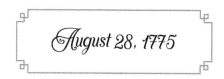

August 28, 1775

Samuel Dow, *who fought at Bunker Hill, wrote to his brother,* **Joseph Dow** *at Standish. Cambridge Camp, August 28, 1775*

Dear Brother,

I embrace the opportunity to write to let you know that I am well and in good health at present thanks be to God for it and I hope this will find you and all our folks well.

I have nothing strange to write you but we are well and hearty at Prospect the most of us have been poorly.

Last week, I was poorly four or five days, it was by having a bad cold but the doctor gave me some harbs that helpt me.

I sent you a letter by Mr. Daniel Illsley and I want to know whether you received it or not. I heard from home last week by Mr. Ingraham but I have had no letter since I came here from home.

I have brought my jacket and shirt and paper, quill, and ink but I don't see that they welcome. Mother has taken a great deal of pains to send Abner some sugar and other things 130 miles, and they got here today. I have thought that she might have sent me something as well as he. I should not a thought that she would have taken so much pains to send a sugar-tit 130 miles when there is enough here.

Shall be very glad to have some things sent for I don't know when we shall get our wages. I cannot tell when I shall come home.

You must not look for us till January if we should live some at Boston, but I remain your loving brother till death.

Samuel Dow

Last Saturday night about two or three thousand of our people went on a hill to entrench about a half mile from the Regulars.

A Sunday morning the Regulars find cannon all day and killed three of our people, two of them had their heads shot off, one of the riflemen had his leg shot off.

Our men are to dig in upon the hill now.

This action was the Naval bombardment of Plough Hill on August 26-27, 1775, the rifleman who lost his leg was Pennsylvania volunteer Billy Simpson, who subsequently died from his wounds.

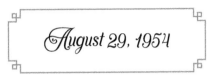

August 29, 1954

The 150th Anniversary of the Old Red Church was celebrated.

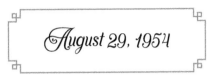

August 30, 1913

The Portland Water District placed a hypochlorite sterilization plant in operation. It was operated until November 18th of that year for experimental purposes.

Below: Hypochlorite tank on Hinkley Brook - Intake in the background

To **James Hasty Jr.** Clerk of the Town of Standish:

Taken up by the subscriber on the 31st day of August last, Damage present on my farm in Standish, one mare of about 12 years-old hath all of a dark color with white face & white hind feet & black mane & tail - with some white spots on her back.

- **Daniel Mitchell**

STANDISH, MAINE

EST

SEPTEMBER

1785

CUMBERLAND COUNTY

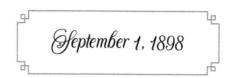

September 1, 1898

"Town of Standish debtor to **Winfield Weeman** for loss of blanket and breaking eggs March 14, 1898 by road being unpassable. $2.50

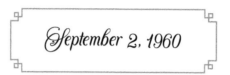

September 2, 1960

Roy Waldron, of Steep Falls, was trapped in his home by a giant swarm of honey bees.

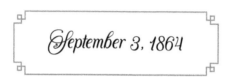

September 3, 1864

FROM THE DIARY OF JOHN P. MOULTON

Warm but Cloudy. In the fore noon did not do much only fuss around the shop. In the afternoon went up to hear Talbot & Dunnell speak, they were damn black and they could not say much for that party. In the eve at home. Had a jaw with **William H. Ward.** He and his wife left town and I hope is to God that they won't come in to it very soon again.

The term "black" here means sullen, dismal or horrible. There is no racial context. Noah Webster's 1839 Dictionary of the American Language

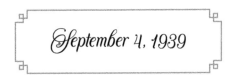

September 4, 1939

FROM THE AUTOGRAPH BOOK OF ARLENE CROWLEY '42 (LEPON)

I have a little garden,
but they have far it is dead.

For I found a bachelor button,
in the black-eyed Susan bed.

Your pal, **Hilda** (Rackliff '40)

Beverly Cushman Francs Beane Phyllis Pratt Alice Edgecomb Bessie Buzzell Miriam Dolloff Nancy Dole

Edna Lewis Arlene Crowley Virginia Smith Agnes Harmon Shirley Estes Marion Gould

Eva Woodbrey Marion Blake Beulah Ricker Patricia Dole Eleanor Lewis

SHS 39-40

Standish High School Girls Basketball 1940

September 5, 1915

THE FIRST ENTRY IN THE CAMP DIARY OF ASA & GENEVA LIBBY DOUGLASS

"At Camp Nephawin for the day: Mrs. and Mrs. **Asa M Douglass, Lloyd Douglass, Marion Douglass,** Mr. **Lewis Douglass,** Mr. & Mrs. **Fred O. Child, Mary Child, Alma Child,** Miss **Mona Emery.**

"Nothing to eat and no place to go so we stopped to supper. Mr. and Mrs. **Fred Libby** and son **Charles** called. Went swimming and spoiled the water. A good time. Asa washed the dinner dishes. Fred was

nursemaid. Lots of real snapping crackers and puddles on the kitchen floor."

The camp still exists, although not in the family, on Thomas Rd Ext. Nephawin is "Spirit of Sleep" or "rest" from the Sokokis; Asa and Geneva has moved from Sebago Lake village to North Gorham Pond the year before; Lloyd Douglass was 3 1/2 and Marion 9 months

Camp Nephawin

Asa Douglass — ?? — Geneva Libby Douglass — Harry Colesworthy — Lloyd Douglass — Alice Douglass Colesworthy — Marion Douglass

September 6, 1881

FROM THE JOURNAL OF EMMA GRAFFAM SHAW

The yellow day was in 1881, Sept. 6th. We had to light the lamp to see to do our work at Bacon Coat Shop. Nearly all day.

The Thumb Fire took place September 5th, 1881 in Michigan. It burned over a million acres in less than a day. In Standish, on September 6th, the sky appeared yellow and twilight appeared at noon due to the soot and ash from the fire which obscured the sun.

W.H. Bacon & Co. Coat Shop

September 7, 1791

Commonwealth of Massachusetts, Cumberland js. To **Daniel Hasty** and **Jonathan Lowell** both of Standish in said county yeoman.

Greetings, Whereas **Job York** of said Standish yeoman has made application to me **John Deane** one of the justices of the peace for the county aforesaid for the appointment of two disinterested judicious persons to apprise the damage that he the said Job has sustained by one horse taken damage pesant? in the said Job's enclosure and impounded as the law directs –– These are therefore in the name oof the said Commonwealth to will and require you the said **Daniel Hasty** and **Jonathan Lowell** upon oath to repair to enclosure of the said Job and there view and estimate the damages done the said Job by the said horse and you are alike required forthwith to repair to the town pound in said Standish and there appraise the said horse at his true value in money according to your best knowledge and judgement and make return of your doing, heron into the Clerk's office of said Standish immediately after your service is performed.

Given under my hand and seal at Standish aforesaid, John Deane, Justice of the Peace.

Cumberland Js., Pursuant to the within warrant, We have appraised the damage that the said Job York has sustained by the said horse to be five shillings and six pence and have appraised the said horse at Eight Shillings. Daniel Hasty, Jonathan Lowell

September 8, 1823

Edward Tompson was granted a license to be a Victualler & Innholder in Standish.

A Victualler provides provisions; he was not licensed to Retail Strong Liquors as that was crossed out.

Edward Tompson ran what became known as the Landmark House on the corner of Northeast Rd. and Ossipee Trail West.

"The Old Landmark"
Home, Inn & Stables of Edward Tompson
(corner of Rt 25 & 35)
Lexington Elms

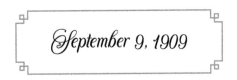

September 9, 1909

Marshall Sanborn and **Irvin Bailey** recently launched their new steam boat which they built in the Saco River, and that afternoon they gave a large number of their friends a ride up the river. The Steamboat is named the "Sokokis".

Portland Evening Express

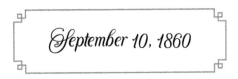

September 10, 1860

FROM THE DIARIES OF JOHN P. MOULTON

Fair and pleasant. **George** and I put up some fence in the morning. Then we went to Town meeting, the Republicans beat us on representative, 27 votes but Naples beat them 30.

He previously noted - September 6, "I joined the independents and we marched around the corner. The Democrats had a mass meeting." and September 8, "In the afternoon was up to the corner to a Republican meeting, we had a good supper given to us by that party."

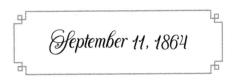

September 11, 1864

FROM THE DIARIES OF JOHN P. MOULTON

Warm and pleasant, In the fore noon was up to the corner fixing to raise a flag. Afternoon went up and raised the flag and had speaking from **H. J. Swasey**, Col. **D. W. Wardwell**, Capt. **Geo. W. Bicknell** & **Edward Swasey**. Had a bully time, about 250 there.

Mr. and Mrs. **Stephen W. Wood** of Steep Falls were recently entertaining a party of friends at Horn Pond. Master **Guy Coolbroth**, a nephew of the hostess, unwilling not to share in the good time, although not invited, traveled the entire distance through the woods, his only protection being his bow and arrow. When asked if he was not frightened, he said "Of course not." He arrived at the cottage in time to take lunch with the rest of the party. As Guy is but five years of age, and the distance 2 1/2 miles, we can but admire the little fellow's courage and perseverance to say the least.

Portland Press Herald

September 13, 1909

The village schools opened in the new school building which is well equipped with all the modern improvements. Miss Annie Dolloff of Standish is the teacher of the grammar grade and Miss Mead of Bridgton of the primary school. They are boarding with Mrs. Alice White.

Portland Evening Express

Albion Howe School

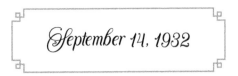

September 14, 1932

Sebago Lake, Maine - Town of Standish School Dept. To Lawrence Sanborn. Sebago Lake Maine - Climbing flag pole and installing new Flag rope - $2.50 at Sebago Lake School.

September 15, 1960

Steep Falls - Coolbroth's Market closed its doors. Opened as Rose's Porter's General Store, the Coolbroth Brothers, **Edwin & Guy** bought the building and opened a grocery store in 1936.

High School commenced on Monday with an attendance of 32. There are nine in the entering class, seven boys and two girls.

September 17, 1870

Formal opening of the stretch of the Portland & Ogdensburg Railroad was marked Sept. 17 by an excursion to the lake by directors of the road and their families, city officials and other guests, who were accompanied by Chandler's Band. They danced on a platform in the grove close to "our great fresh water reservoir," strolled along the shore, picnicked on the grass, "rushed for a bowl of Perry's Chowder," and enjoyed an hours sail aboard a steamer.

Quoth the editor of the Portland Transcript: "The spot has all the attractions to make it a great pleasure resort for our people, and Sebago will yet be to Portland what Bedford Basin is to Halifax." We know nothing about Bedford Basin, but the editor is right in his prediction that the lake would become a great pleasure resort.

Sebago Lake Station c. 1870's

**Steamer Mount Pleasant
Portland and Ogdensburg Railroad**

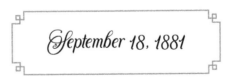

September 18, 1881

SEBAGO LAKE CONCERTS

The sacred concerts took place at Sebago Lake yesterday and a large crowd was present to listen to Chandler's delightful music. It is estimated that there were over two thousand people present. Eighteen cars containing over a thousand people went from this city and six cars from Upper Bartlett. Good order prevailed throughout the day. The return train arrived here at 7:30 last evening.

Portland Daily Press

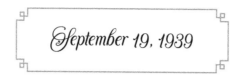

September 19, 1939

FROM THE DIARY OF GILBERT MOULTON

Stormed hard all day and is raining hard tonight. At home all day and evening. **Edward** and **Belle** came this afternoon. 60 above tonight. There was a very sudden death this noon down to the High School. One of **Amos Woodbrey**'s girls (**Cloris**) 14 years old, dropped dead. It was her first year in the school.

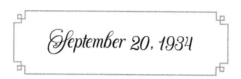

September 20, 1934

The Portland Tourist Company charged the Town of Standish for the following:

- To third class passage, Boston to Galway - **Irene Florence Davis** and Master **John F. Davis** - 1 1/2 at $84.50 = **$126.75**

- US Revenue Tax, 1 @ $5.00 and 1 @ $3.00 = **$8.00**

- US Passport including cost of money order covering Master **John F. Davis** - **$10.10**

- Irish Free State visa on US passport of Master **John F. Davis** - **$10.00**

- Irish Free State passport covering **Irene Florence Davis** - **$3.54**

- Special toll call to the Passport agent in connection with passport covering **John Francis Davis** - **$1.65**

- Cost of new birth certificate, obtained from the City Clerk, Westbrook - **$ .50**

- Cost of special messenger from Portland to the office of the City Clerk, Westbrook and return, in connection with obtaining new birth certificate, this being in accordance with instructions received from the passport officials - **$ .75**

- Toll call to the Passport Agent respecting proceeding with the issuance of emergency passport covering **John Francis Davis** - **$1.65**

Total $162.94

No other information on this has been found - Very Curious! There was only one Davis, Walter, listed in the 1930 Census. Even more Curious!

Daniel Marrett was ordained at the First Parish Church of Standish. He was the third minister. He received members from Standish and adjoining towns. Because of dismissals, excommunications, removals and deaths of members of the church, the parish collector found trouble collecting Parson Marrett's salary, which was fixed at £88 per annum.

Standish Congregational Church 1877
Interior

A Town warrant was issued "to see if the town will raise a bounty of three hundred dollars for each soldier who has been or may be drafted from this town under the last call for troops and who shall himself or his substitute be mustered into the service of the United States, as a part of this town's quota.

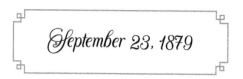

REPUBLICAN JOLLIFICATION AT STANDISH, SEBAGO, SEPTEMBER 23 (TUESDAY)

The Republicans of Standish and vicinity had a grand jollification meeting here Saturday to celebrate their recent victory in the state and to rejoice with their Lord over the election of their Representative, in this class, to the Legislature. They had torchlights, music, and fireworks, while a canon placed on Davis' Hill added greatly to the general effect. Short pithy speeches were made by A. G. Bradstreet, Esq., Hon. **H. B. Cleaves** and **B. T. Chase**, Esq., after which oysters were provided for all, and a more substantial supper for those who wished, while a dance in the hall closed the celebration. Fully 500 people were present and all went home thoroughly convinced that they had had a good time.

Portland Daily Press

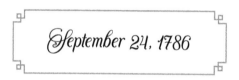

Peter Moulton carted lumber & men to Portland four consecutive days to pay the Beef Tax execution. He was paid £2...6....0 for his services. *(2 pounds, 6 shillings). It is not recorded whether the lumber paid the tax or the lumber was sold to pay the tax.*

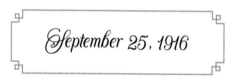

The Town of Standish was billed $1.00 by the Cumberland County Power & Light Company for electricity usage by the Town Hall for the previous month. The billing was the minimum as the Town used less than one KWH (Kilowatt hour) during that period of time.

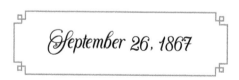

We the undersigned Republicans of the Town of Standish having been nominated as candidates to be supported for town officers at the coming annual election by a Democratic caucus and the same having been done without our previous knowledge or consent do under any and all circumstances decline serving as said candidates - **Joseph S. Tompson, William Rich, Harvey Wescott**

THE ninth annual exhibition of the Gorham and Standish Farmers' Club, will be held on the grounds of the Club's trotting park, in the big tent, at North Gorham, on Tuesday, October 12, 1869.

The notice announces the several committees, made up from the substantial farmers of these agricultural towns. This exhibition heretofore has been a great success, has attracted a large crowd, and been productive of much good. The present programme is full of interest, and the arrangements under the direction of its efficient chairman, Samuel Dingley, Esq., will be perfect.

Portland Daily Press

Bonny Eagle High School was dedicated.

Harvey Foster received a Purple Heart Medal for wounds received in action during WWI. He was a messenger on the front lines, a constant target when moving outside the trenches.

The town of Standish received a bill from the Western Maine Power Company, formerly the Limerick Water and Electric Company, for $76 for street light service in the village of Steep Falls, for the three months ending September 30.

STANDISH, MAINE · EST · OCTOBER · 1785 · CUMBERLAND COUNTY

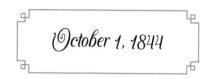

October 1, 1844

FROM GARDNER DENNETT'S ACCOUNT LEDGER

James W. Emery purchased 3 5/8 yards of Alpaca for $1.20 and 3 yards of Cambric for 24¢. Edward Peabody purchased a churn for $2.50.

The churn was a butter churn but there is no indication of what form it was. The Alpaca came from Peru probably by way of England where it was woven into fabric, but this predates the Titus Salt 1853 revolution in weaving Alpaca. Cambric is a light weight plain-weave fabric made of linen or cotton.

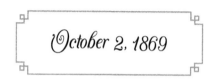

October 2, 1869

State Pension Office, Augusta: Selectmen, Standish, Gentlemen:

In the case of **William Wescott Jr.** - guardian of organ children of **Ai Bolton.** I wish you two forward me a copy of his letter of appointment as guardian - Also inform me if you are sure as to the amount of Mil. Pension these children receive - The amount is given as $8 per month in the application. Please attend to this request immediately & much oblige.

Yours very truly, **Henry C. Reed**

Ai Bolton, 25th Maine Infantry, died in Standish 4/4/1867 as a result of disease contracted in the service. The 25th Maine Infantry of 993 men was assigned to the defense of the Capital and was encamped on Arlington Heights, in the front line of defense. The regiment saw no action. 25 men died of disease while serving.

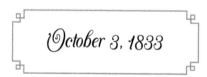

October 3, 1833

Sir, We the undersigned take this opportunity to inform you that we never did, do not, nor shall we ever (unless our minds become materially altered) consider ourselves members of this or any other Parish liable to taxation so long as wood grows or waters run, and remain your humble servants:

Albert Sanborn, Warren Sanborn, Josiah Mayo, Alonzo Mayo, Johnson Sanborn.

We the above names persons hereby request you as clerk of the First Parish in Standish, to cause our names to be stricken from the list of this liable to be taxed, in said Parish if they be bourne on said list - to **Thomas Cram Jr.**

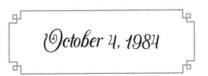

There will be a special town meeting at the George E. Jack school gymnasium, on October 13 at 1pm to present a report on the feasibility study undertaken to see if there is a need for a new municipal center, and act on the acceptance of the unused Johnson land and buildings.

Ad in the Portland Press Herald

Town Pump 1879

Sawyer Coat Factory on right
"Old Landmark" on left
Looking toward Sebago Lake along Northeast Rd.

October 5, 1935

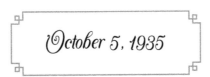

FROM THE DIARY OF GILBERT MOULTON

Clowdy and cool. **Ed** and **Belle**, **Bertha** and I went out riding today. Went up to their camp in Milan in the afternoon. Was over in Randolph and got caught in a snowstorm. We saw some of the most beautiful scenery that I have ever seen.

They had traveled to Berlin NH the day before, leaving at 9:50 am and arriving at 2 pm. They went to the pictures that evening. The next day they drove up to the airport. They returned home on the 7th.

FROM THE STORE LEDGER OF LEMUEL RICH & SON

Sold to:

- N. E. Sawyer - vinegar 20¢

- Helen Hooper - Sugar 27¢, cloves 10¢

- D. W. Stanly - Molasses 24¢, Sugar 18¢, Nutmeg 8¢, lard 33¢

- Mary A. Blake - Corned Beef 23¢, Potatoes 28¢, crackers 15¢, fish 14 ¢

- G. H. Moulton - 1 box salt 22¢

- W. S. Hanscom - 1/2 lb. tea 25¢, 1 lb. coffee 25¢, lard 40¢, Molasses 24¢, Raisins 15¢

- Portland Water Co. - 7 lbs. Nails 21¢

- Luther Blake - Molasses 20¢, Beans 20¢, oil 7¢, starch 4¢, meal 9¢, crackers 15¢

- E. Libby - 2" spikes 6¢

- Thomas Moses - Sugar 36¢

- C. H. Cole - Lard 39¢

- Fanny Marean - Sugar 18¢, eggs 5¢

- Charles F. Parker - 2 1/4 lasting 90¢, 1 1/2 S. lining 23¢

- W. L. Bacon - Mustard sauce 20¢

- Thomas Welch - Barrel Flour $6.50

- George P. Bennett - Pants $2.50, matches 9¢

- Lennie Davis - Gloves $1.00, shade 8¢

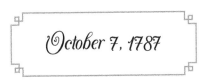

October 7, 1787

A town warrant was issued to meet "To see what method said town will take to build a school house or houses." *(It was still on the agenda 6 months later.)*

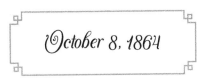

October 8, 1864

After being captured on May 3, 1863 and held as a POW at Chancellorville, then paroled, **Napoleon Bonaparte Abbott**, a sergeant with Company H, 17th Maine Infantry, was wounded at the Battle of the Wilderness on May 7, 1864, Then wounded at the Battle of Petersburg on October 7th, 1864 and killed in action on the following day, October 8th.

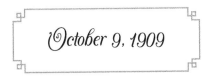

October 9, 1909

FROM THE DIARY OF GILBERT MOULTON

Pleasant and warm. Was on the route until 3 pm, around home rest of day and evening. **Joe Knight**'s buildings was burned tonight. Loss $10,000, 4 horses, 2 hogs, 2 heifers, 65 tons Hay, 20 tons straw, 600 bushels oats, 700 bushels potatoes and all of his farming tools was burned.

Jo Knight's place owned at the time this picture was taken by Orrie Bragdon and Charles Harmon. It later burned and was replaced by the home of Arthur C. and Louise Harmon

Pavilion, Cottage Burn at Steep Falls. Wildwood pavilion, adjoining dining room and three room cottage, a popular wayside resort on the Pequawket Trail about a mile from this village, were destroyed by fire of unknown origin. Mr. and Mrs. **Theodore Marean**, of Oak Hill in Standish, place the damage at $9,000 with very little insurance. They were temporarily overcome by their loss and a physician attended the couple. The buildings had been unoccupied since the close of the Summer.

Wildwood was located on Pequawket Trail about a mile from Steep Falls village and was very popular. Unfortunately, we do not have a photo of Wildwood. Below is Portland St., Steep Falls.

Fred Marean has a nice lot of potatoes this Fall. One day last week, three men dug 150 bushels by hand.

Portland Evening Express

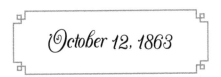

October 12, 1863

To the Treasurer of the Town of Standish:

Pay to **James R. Rand** on order in ten years with interest annually for said time and no longer, unless demanded of you thereafter at your office, Three Hundred Dollars as bounty for service as a Soldier, accepted and liable to do duty under a law of Congress called the Conscription Act.

By authority of votes passed at the town meeting held Oct. 2nd 1863: **Joseph Sanborn, Ebenezer Moulton, Asa Berry**; Selectmen of Standish.

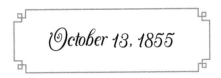

October 13, 1855

Know all men by these presents, that I **John Smith Jr.** of Standish in the County of Cumberland in consideration of one hundred and fifty dollars paid by **Lemuel Rich** 3rd of Standish in said county = the receipt whereof I do hereby acknowledge do hereby give, grant, bargain, and sell unto him the same Lemuel Rich 3rd and his heirs and assigns forever, the dwelling house now in the progress of building, on land said Lemuel Rich 3rd which he purchased of **Woodbrey Storer** Esq. which said land is now occupied by me - the said John Smith Jr. To have and to hold said house to him the said Lemuel Rich 3rd his heirs and assigns forever, and I do avouch myself to be the true and lawful owner of said house and have in myself good right and lawful authority to sell and convey said house to said Lemuel Rich 3rd to hold as aforesaid and that I will warrant and forever defend said house unto him the said Lemuel Rich 3rd against the lawful claims and demands of all persons. In witness whereof the said John Smith Jr. have hereunto set my mark and seal.

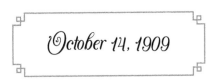

October 14, 1909

Loyalty Camp, No. 1941, of Royal Neighbors met in regular session. The entertainment committee consisted of Mrs. **May Ridlon**, Miss **Helen Marr**, and **James Ridlon**. After the regular business was transacted a baked bean supper was served, which was followed by a **Hard Times** Social. Stories of **Hard Times** were told and the prize was given to Master **Clarence Hanscom**.

Portland Evening Express

Equipment was moved into place for the abutment work of the new steel and cement bridge over the Saco river. It is a WPA project. The new bridge will be about 20 feet at the left of the site of the bridge washed away in the Spring floods. It will extend 200 feet on each side from the river bank and will be four feet higher than the old one.

Baldwin, Gentlemen, I wish to know what action has ben maid in regard to my colts ingress received in that bridge. I am a wair that I have laid the damages much smaller that thay rearly air she does not get ainy better. I think the kne is vers than it was when you saw it. Yours with Respects in haste L. A. Dow —- heare is a part of a leter & recured from Mr. Rice. He was with me when the colt got hirt. Oct. 1st 1865, Friend Leander, I received your lines last night and will write immediately don't know but it will be to late for yauss has been on the road eight days. You wrote in regard to your horse had supposed was settled long before this for Dean see no chance for dispute in relation to that bridge it being such as is accident that it was an old rotten affair. I can see no reasons for disbelieving that there was no hole before we drove over to be sure I did not see it an account of such a cloud of dust all the way you know. I hope you will not meet with too much of a loss for I should think you had offered to settle on more reasonable terms than you could afford although if she gets entirely over it you will consider yourself lucky of course. you know we thought the bruise on her leg might not prove to be serious. She must have wrenched her shoulder when she fell.

The 3 1/2 ton Pumper recently purchased by the town for fire protection was tested, when 500 gallons of water per minute was pumped from Tucker brook to the residence of L. A. Pitts in the Coopertown section of Steep Falls, a distance of 2,400 feet. Below, one of the fire trucks in service in Standish.

The first water flowed from Sebago Lake to Portland. (see Nov 18)

At right, the Portland Water Company intake, 1916.

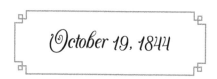

At a Legal meeting of the members of the First Parish of Standish. ... 2nd. Voted that the assessors be instructed to provide what wood is necessary for warming this house this Winter. 4th. Voted to tender to the Washingtonians of Standish the use of this house at all times when it does not interrupt with religious services held here.

The Washingtonians, the Washingtonian Movement or the Washingtonian Temperance Society, was founded in 1840 by six alcoholics at Chase's Tavern in Baltimore, Maryland. The idea was that by working together, they could keep each other sober. The goal was total abstinence. Similar to Alcoholics Anonymous, it predates AA by 100 years.

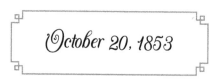

Know all men by these presents that I **Mylberry Harmon** of Standish in the County of Cumberland State of Maine in Consideration of the sum of thirty dollars in hand paid by **Ebenezer Moulton** of said town I do sell and convey unto said Moulton my red Mare being about nine years old and being the same that I had of **James Palmer** of Buxton in the County of York.

(These sales were received and recorded by the Town Clerk.)

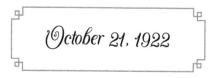

The Standish Telephone Company billed the Selectman's office for a Toll Call to Raymond, 15¢, the call was made by 8-2 to 24-2.

(All out of town calls were toll calls, 8-2 & 24-2 identified the caller and receiver of the call.)

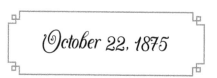

Child for Adoption.

A SMART, bright, healthy boy eight months old will be given to some good family who may be able and willing to give him a good home. Apply to Overseers of Poor, Standish, Me. oct12dtf

Portland Daily Press

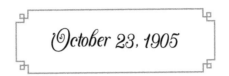

October 23, 1905

FROM THE DAIRY OF GILBERT MOULTON

Pleasant, was on the route until 3 - PM, around home rest of day and evening. They broke into the depot today and blowed the safe all to peaces and only got $1.03 for their trouble.

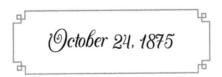

October 24, 1875

Steep Falls, Selectmen of Standish,

The family I refer to have been until within a few years residents of Bridgton but have been moving quite often since and I presume have not gained a residence any place else: I was called the first time to see the wife suffering from congestion of the lungs but she soon got over that, but she soon got cold again and as she was nursing a child at that time, her next trouble was inflammation of breast which proved to be very severe, and I could only relieve her of intense suffering by some palliative measure for the time and let it come to a point suitable for the lance, and thus it went from bad to worse for three weeks, and I had to attend it to keep the intense pain as quiet as I could hoping that every visit would be the last till I had been up there to see her wants sixteen times, a distance of about a mile and a half and sometimes I was obliged to remain there a long time and use much medicine and I have only charges seventy five cents a visit. They are a very poor and needy family and he cannot pay his bills, so I have made a town charge of it, and hope it will be convenient for you to collect your pay from Bridgton and remit to me soon. I am very confident that this Kelley's father now lives on the Bridgton town farm. As to this case I have told you as near as I could, all the circumstances, so you might know that I did not make out an unjust bill for my work.

As to the Ranolds boy from Limerick that was injured at Andrew Ridlon's stable. Mr. Ridlon told me he notified you very early and said you told him that his bill & the doctors bill would be paid all right so I did not notify you of it. My bill there was for six visits ($5.50) but I suppose likely you will pay that but I do not know. Yours, **J. B. Andrews** M.D. Steep Falls

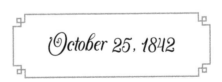

October 25, 1842

Know all men by these Presents that I **James W. Emery** of Standish in the County of Cumberland and State of Maine - Tailor - for a good and valuable consideration to me in hand, well and truly paid, at or before the signing, sealing and delivery of these presents, by **Samuel Phinney** of said Standish - Blacksmith - the receipt thereof I the said James do hereby acknowledge, have granted, bargained and sold, and by these presents, do grant, bargain and sell unto the said Samuel Phinney a certain Blacksmith shop, standing on land this day conveyed by the said Samuel to me in the southeasterly side of the road leading from Standish Village to Buxton - And the said Samuel agrees to remove the said shop from the said land by the first day of April next. ...

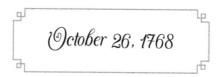

October 26, 1768

John Tompson was ordained for service in Pearsontown. He was the first minister of Pearsontown.

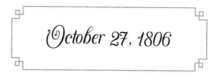

October 27, 1806

A warrant for the November 3rd Town meeting: 2. To see if the town will vote to repair the meetinghouse in said town; 3. To vote money to repair said meetinghouse; 8. To see if the town will vote to remove the old Meetinghouse & erect said house into a Town house & selectmen's office or otherwise disposed said house as said Town & the first Parish or proprietors of the Pews shall agree.

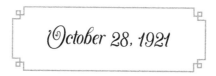

October 28, 1921

The Bradbury and Lowell Houses burned. Located on Main Street next to the Dolloff Store, Standish Hardware is now located on these sites.

Bradbury · Lowell · Dolloff Store

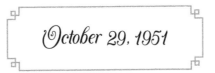

October 29, 1951

The first classes started at the George E. Jack School.

George E. Jack School

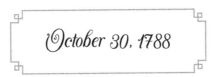

October 30, 1788

Sargent Shaw was paid Four Pounds, Fourteen Shillings and Five Pence for his work on the roads in Standish, signs by **George Freeman** and **Josiah Shaw**, Selectmen.

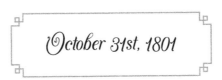

October 31st, 1801

An order was written to pay Rev. **Daniel Marrett** Two Hundred Sixty Six dollars for one year's salary as Minister of the 1st Parish Church of Standish. It was signed by **Peter Moulton**, **John Deane** & **Daniel Hasty**; selectmen of Standish

As the congregation of the 1st Parish (Old Red Church) waned, it became increasing difficult to raise the funds needed to pay Daniel Marrett's salary.

STANDISH, MAINE

EST

NOVEMBER

1785

CUMBERLAND COUNTY

The Highland House at South Standish burned down. It was a total loss. Built by **Simon Moulton**, run by **Edgar S.** Norton, it was owned by **James Douglass** of Gorham when it burned.

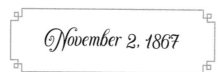

FROM THE DIARY OF JOHN P. MOULTON

A very windy day. We started in the lead at 6, got up Co-ling?? beach at 2. Loaded up all of the wood that we was going to carry to Portland and started for home when opposite smooth ledge a squall struck us and carried away our fine sail and we sailed down under Indian Island under bare poles laid there all night.

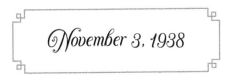
FROM THE STANDISH HIGH SCHOOL AUTOGRAPH BOOK OF ARLENE CROWLEY (LEPON) CLASS OF 1942

They sat on the porch at midnight;
Their lips were tightly pressed;

The old man gave the signal:
And the bulldog did the rest.

Your Classmate, **Virginia Smith**

Arlene Crowley '42

Virginia Smith '42

November 4, 1910

MORE MEN ARE WANTED

Contractors are Pushing Work on New Dam at Bonny Eagle

Work Will Require Two Years for Its Completion

The contractors who have the contract for the high dam which is to be built at Bonny Eagle on the Saco River are pushing the work as rapidly as possible, being somewhat bothered in getting sufficient help. At present, there are over 100 men at work on the job and it is the desire of the contractors that they might increase this number to 300 or more. The completion of the work it is expected will occupy two years. A large cookhouse and dining room have been erected near the river and the men are very comfortably located in these quarters. A number of workmen from this city have been up to look over the prospects for a winter's job and several have expressed their intention of securing work there.

Up to date, the work has been largely of a preparatory nature, although quite a little excavating has been done for the foundations of the dam. This is to be a huge affair, something like 50 feet in height and over 300 feet in length. It will flow an area of several square miles.

The work at this point includes not only the building of this dam, but the installation of an electrical power plant capable of developing several thousand horse power. The power thus developed, it is said, although not authoritatively, will be largely used in Portland, either in the street car traffic or for manufacturing purposes. The plant when complete, will be one of the finest in the state and will represent the expenditure of many thousands of dollars.

The Saco River, at this point, is particularly well adapted for the purpose of developing water power, as the banks are comparatively close together, which obviates the necessity of building a very long dam. Just below the location of the power plant, the river is contracted between steep gorges and rushes foaming onward for nearly half a mile ere it again resumes its placid flow. It is a picturesque spot, which will not be enhanced from an artistic standpoint by the work which is being done there, but the material benefits will doubtless far outweigh the loss of its wild beauty.

The Lewiston Evening Journal

FROM THE OXFORD DEMOCRAT

The establishment of **Henry B. Hartford**, including a general store, dwelling house, stable, carriage house, post office, sale workshop, and printing office, at Standish Corner, was destroyed by fire Monday morning, entailing a loss that must exceed $10,000 and upon which there was an insurance approximating $6,000. The building consumed by the fire occupied a square of land in the center of the little village of Standish, covering nearly half an acre of land. The loss is a severe one to the community. About 15 people are thrown out of employment besides those who did outside work for the sale work firm.

Henry B. Hartford

TWO FATALLY INJURED WHEN FREIGHT CRASHES TEAM

STEEP FALLS, Nov. 7 (Special to the Express-Advertiser).—Mrs. **Robert Ridlon**, 39, died Tuesday evening as a result of an accident at the Maine Central Crossing in this village late Tuesday and Mrs. **Charles Sanborn**, 57, who was with her, died this morning. The horse they were driving was killed, the wagon shattered into a total wreck and the women, hurled 40 to 50 feet by the impact, escaped instant death only by a miracle. Mrs. Ridlon was unconscious from the time she landed in the door yard of Mrs. **Minnie Ridlon** on the northeast side of the track and she died shortly after 10 in the evening. Dr. **George I. Geer** medical examiner, pronounced the cause of death shock and internal hemorrhage with concussion of the brain. Her left leg was broken below the knee, scrapes cuts and abrasions were numerous all over her body and it was impossible to accomplish anything for her relief.

Mrs. Sanborn suffered fractures of both legs at the ankle, there was a deep cut in one thigh and a score of cuts and bruises showed that she was injured fatally also. It was thought last night that she would not survive and she passed away at 3 o'clock. Dr. **Lorenzo Norton** of Mattocks who was called was in constant attendance on the two women, at the bedside of Mrs. Sanborn ever since the death of Mrs. Ridlon. Dr. **Samuel G. Sawyer** of Cornish was called to assist him also.

The two women started to drive from their homes on the Portland road, so-called, to K. of P. Hall to attend a social and even though it is but a short distance, perhaps a third of a mile, decided to ride over. The horse was owned by Mr. Ridlon, was docile and fearless, being driven for several years by his wife. They drove over the crossing on the main highway which is on the route to Mattocks without noticing any signs of a train approaching, drove in rear of the passenger station to the road leading toward Limington and failed to stop when a warning whistle was blown as the train neared the first crossing. This is 300 yards or such a matter from the northern or upper crossing.

Three times the engineer, making his first trip over the line as a driver, it is said, blew the whistle, short shrill blasts, as he had noticed the wagon and women occupants.

He applied the brakes, but the heavy freight special scarcely was retarded in its speed and the rig was hit squarely, both horse and wagon being hurled and rolled off the rails, the wagon occupants tossed high in the air and to the northeast side of the iron.

No one other than the engine crew saw the accident at the instant it happened and the first person to reach the scene was **Harry Ridlon**, brother of the dead woman's husband. He ran to their aid and a score or more gathered in two or three minutes. Brakes were applied hard to the train which stopped after running more than its full length past the crossing.

There is a clear view up the track for a distance of about 250 or 300 yards where the track makes a sharp curve and even down the line toward Portland a straight stretch for two miles or more is in full view but at times freight cars on the siding and the buildings at the station are obstructions and it was in this direction that the train came from at high speed. To see full well, the women must have had to turn and look over their shoulders when close to the iron as the highway and railroad do not form a right angle at the crossing.

The two women lived nearly opposite the village library, with but one house between the Sanborn and Ridlon residences. They had lived many years in the village within plain sight of the lower crossing and by daily association kept track of train schedules. This train was a special freight, following the noon passenger train that runs through the mountain. They had no intimation that there was any danger undoubtedly.

Mrs. Ridlon was Sarah Robinson of Gray, an adopted daughter, at the time of her marriage 16 or 17 years ago. She had two sisters and a brother and her mother was living the last time she heard from her relatives but her adoption in her infancy led to dissolution of the family as no definite knowledge is available as to their whereabouts.

She was a church member, belonged also to the Pythian Sisterhood, was active in various village entertainment and social affairs, and was well liked by all who knew her.

Mrs. Sanborn lived in her girlhood in East Limington and in Steep Falls since her first marriage, there being two daughters, Mrs. Emma Hunkins of that village and Mrs. William Clark of Portland. She was conscious ever since she was hurt and her injuries occasioned her most acute suffering.

Despite the traffic over this Highway, the main line through Gorham, Standish and Baldwin, thence on to summer resorts on the west side of Sebago Lake and in the mountains, accidents have been almost unknown at either of these crossings. This fatality was on the lesser traveled road as the railroad really divides the village which is divided again by the Saco River, Standish, and Limington town boundary at this point.

Passenger service on the Portland and Ogdensburg
Railroad started at Steep Falls.

On election night, Fred Marean's Hotel, Store and stables burned in Steep Falls, the flames being fanned by high winds. The damage was $18,000. (Photos at right.)

MAREAN'S HOTEL STEEP FALLS, ME. 75.

1912

MAIN ST. STANDISH ME. 75.

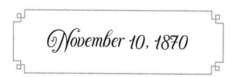

November 9, 1859

Manchester NH - Dear Brother, I seat myself to pen a few lines to you but without pleasure to me - to let you know that my wife is dead and buried. She was sick but one week and one day. I have written to Charles to four different places but could not find him nor heard from him. John, I should have written to you before this time but I did not think she was dangerous until two or three days before she died. It is hard for me to not have emmey or her folks here with me. John tell mother that she was willing to die and called me to her bed and told me that she hated to leave me and little Bub and wanted me to take good care of the baby. The baby is very sick now, I don't know as he shall live long - Martha was taken a ??? and a bad disease. I had two doctors, Dr. Back and Dr. Tewksbury. They called it conssunton (consumption) Martha died Friday November the 4 and was buried Sunday the 6. I have broke up keeping house and gone to Boarding out with Martha, and the Baby is with me. **George Whittier** - Write soon.

Martha Ann Whittier *died at 26 of Cholera Morbus from the death certificate. She was married to* **George W. Whittier**. *Brother John was* **John Otis** *of Standish*

November 10, 1870

To the Selectmen of Standish,

Sirs, I have learned subsequent to the adjourned meeting of this town that I was then and there chosen Constable and Collector for this town for the ensuing year. The offer which I most respectfully decline unless the town will pay at least 2 1/2 ¢ on the dollar for collecting.

Yours, **James L. Paine**

November 11, 1805

It was voted at a town meeting to raise 175 Dollars for the purpose of erecting a schoolhouse in the 2nd District.

The second district is located on Standish Neck. This school would predate the Harding school on the corner of the White's Bridge road and Route 35.

Ivory Morse — Flora Lamb Teacher — Addie Chaplin — Will Wescott — Maud Meserve — Leon Blake — Dwight Morse — Kate Libby — Nell Gilman — Wilbur Rogers — Bert Libby

P2021-002-003

Harding School 1889

November 12, 1793

The Town of Standish was billed 0...8....0 (8 shillings) by **Peter Moulton** for Perambulating the Town line.

A CURIOUS STORY.

A young man about 17 years of age, **Libby** by name, attended meeting at York's Corner, Standish, last Sunday evening, as all young men in' that neighborhood should. During the services; he left the house to get a drink of water. As he left the church, two men approached him to inquire the way to **Abraham Came**'s house, and offered to pay him liberally if he would go with them in a covered carriage and show them the were coming. They were coming "right back," and would bring him with them. Having in prospect a generous fee, he consented to show them the way. After entering the carriage, one of the men placed his hand over Libby's mouth to prevent any outcry, while the other ransacked his pocket, and took from him his wallet and a knife. The men were disguised as negroes, and threatened if he resisted to kill him. After taking all the young man had in his pockets, they drove to the edge of a thick forest in Waterborough, near Carle's Corner, where one of the men loft to take care of the horse and carriage, while the other carried the young man quite a distance into the woods, and erected a shanty of boughs for the accommodation of his prisoner. The food of the young man was crust of bread and cold water. Monday afternoon as the keeper returned with some water for his prisoner, the prisoner managed to "hit him a clip" in the head, which felled him, and after "putting his boots" into him several times, he escaped, and after wandering some time in the woods, he succeeded in finding his way out, and reached his home at York's Corner, late Monday night, pretty well exhausted by his treatment and his travels. The above is all the young man can tell about the matter.

The men returned the wallet to Libby, but not his knife.

The Portland Argus

South Standish
York's Corner

Left: Tavern converted to a home, containing So. Standish P.O.
Right: Jeremiah Libby's Home; Upper Right: Carriage Shop

P2002-50y

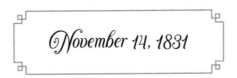

November 14, 1831

To **Oliver Frost**, Town Treasurer or his Successor in that office pay to Thomas Shaw three dollars being for Powder furnished the town. Selectmen of Standish: **Benjamin Poland, Benjamin Chadbourne, Jabez Dow**

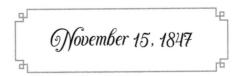

November 15, 1847

FROM THE STORE LEDGER OF GARDNER DENNETT

- **Simeon Mansfield** purchased 2 quarts of sperm oil;
- **Joseph Chase** purchased 2 yards Tweed, 2 3/4 yards of Satinett, 1 yard of Tweed, 2 yards of Lindsay Plaid, 1 3/4 yards of Celatia, 1 1/2 yards of Cambrick, 1 3/4 yards of Canvass, 2 3/4 yards of Sheeting, 1/2 yard Drilling, 12 Buttons, 20 small buttons, 12 pant buttons, 6 sheets wadding, 2 st Twist, 4 sk. Silk, 12 sk. Threads, 1/2 oz linen thread. He spent a total of $7.17.

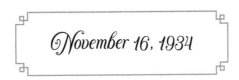

November 16, 1934

FROM THE DIARY OF GILBERT MOULTON

Pleasant and warmer. Went down to Westbrook in the forenoon, at home in the afternoon. Bertha and I went up to Richville in the evening to the Whist party, got home at 12PM.

Joe Martin fell from the Hay mow and broke his elbow and hurt his head very bad, they took him to the Hospital in Portland.

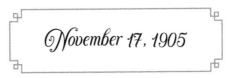

November 17, 1905

Italian's Bail is Defaulted. Bondsmen of Carmillo Lozzi in Liquor Case Must Make Good Bonds of $700. **Carmillo Lozzi**, the Italian who was arrested at Steep Falls, Tuesday, on a charge of the illegal possession of liquor and whose case was continued this morning, failed to make his appearance in court and his bail of $700 was ordered defaulted. His bondsmen were **Barbato Napolitano** and **Bartolomeo Erasmo**. The officers seized several barrels of beer from Lozzi at the time of his arrest. It is alleged that Lozzi was selling beer to a gang of Italians working on the foundation of a paper mill at Steep Falls. Complaint was made by **George Johnson** of Standish who, after drinking beer which he purchased from Lozzi, was robbed of $100 in the camp

Portland Paper

The Portland Water Company announced that water began flowing from Sebago lake to Portland through a 20 inch cement lined steel water main into a reservoir on Bramhall street. Photo below taken in 1882 shows a large break in the Bramhall reservoir.

Samuel Phinney, Bot at Auction: 230 lb. Old Mill Saws, $5.75; 27 lbs. Tyre nails. .95; 45 lb. Old Steel, 1.35; 4 pr Tongs, .50; 138 lbs. Heading tools, 9.60; 158 lbs. Anvils at 9 1/4/lb., 14.61; 102 lbs. anvil @3 1/4 /lb., 3.32; 1 pair Bellows, 7.00; Lot unfinished work, 1.07; 8 drawing knives, 1.00; pointing block, .30: total $49.06 **David Hayes Adm.**

The 2nd Baptist Church was organized at Oak Hill led by Elders **Walter B. Parker** & **Orison Gammon**. Initial members were **John Rand** & **Nancy Rand**, **James N. Rand** & **Harriet Rand**, **Lewis Rand**.

November 21, 1935

A fire destroyed the Androscoggin Pulp Mill in Steep Falls. The mill was purchased in 1934 by Cumberland County Power and Light Company when it took over the water rights.

November 22, 1855

FROM THE DIARY OF JOHN P. MOULTON

Windy and Cold. Was in Biddeford. Went out on the streets in the morning. Did not see Olive while there. This was Thanksgiving. Had a sleigh ride.

They had quite a bit of snow the day before. Took them three hours to travel to Biddeford and four hours to get home the 23rd. John & Sarah went shopping before leaving on the 23rd.

Biddeford 1870's

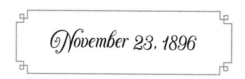

November 23, 1896

One of the first three Rural Delivery Routes in Maine was established with Mr. **Gilbert Moulton** as the first Rural Carrier.

From the Dedication of the New Sebago Lake Post Office on August 20, 1967

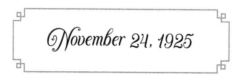

November 24, 1925

Town of Standish, Cumberland County Power and Light Company Electric Bill for Standish High School from October 26th to November 24th: 10 Kilowatt Hours; 80¢

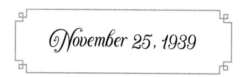

November 25, 1939

FROM THE DIARY OF GILBERT MOULTON OF SEBAGO LAKE VILLAGE

The worst storm for the winter. It began to snow yesterday afternoon and did not let up any until this noon and the wind has blown a gail all day and is blowing very hard tonight. The roads are drifted very bad with the thermometer has not been above 14 all day, and is 10 above tonight. The roads are so bad, Alice and Bob could not go home.

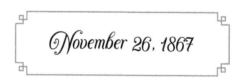

November 26, 1867

FROM THE DIARY OF JOHN P. MOULTON

Foggy day. I started this morning for Portland with **Levi S. Davis** at 3 o'clock. got in about 8. Went in as Grand Juror but was excused because the venerie(?) was not right. Came out also with Levi S. Davis - very muddy traveling, was not very well, had a bad cold.

That's 3am! The trip to Portland from Sebago Lake Village, approximately 25 miles, took 5 hours in 1867.

Venerie was probably Voir Dire, the jury selection process of questioning potential jurors.

The Oak Hill Chapel of the Free Will Baptist Church opened. The church, on Oak Hill Road, has since become a residence.

Oak Hill Chapel

November 28, 1916

Standish High school placed an order with H. H. Hay Sons for chemicals and supplies to equip the Chemistry Laboratory at the new High School at Sebago Lake. It was probably one of several orders for chemistry alone. Included were test tubes, funnels, beakers, evaporating dishes, pneumatic troughs, wide mouth bottles thistle tubes, blow pipes, deflagrating spoons, corks, rubber stoppers, reagent bottles for acids and bases, Electrolysis apparatus and chemicals: Potassium Chromate, Potassium Dichromate, Potassium Ferricyanide, Potassium Ferrocyanide, Potassium Nitrate & Potassium Hydroxide; Sodium Sulfate, Sodium Carbonate, Sodium Hydroxide; Ether, granulated Zinc, Silver Nitrate and more.

Most of these chemicals would not be found in most high school chemistry labs today. The Chromates, Dichromates, Ferri- & Ferrocyanides are toxic and carcinogenic. The hydroxides are highly caustic (Lye) and ether is extremely flammable. Ether was used as an anesthetic.

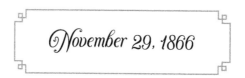

November 29, 1866

Saco, Overseers of the Poor of Standish, Gents, You wrote us that a Mrs. Levitt belonging to our town has become Cheergulele in your town. Will you write us and tell what the bill is and whether She can be moved or not. Yours with Respect, **Charles Hill**

Cheergulele is one of the oddest words I've run across. Looking at the original script, the word is clearly "Cheergulele" but the word actually is probably "Chargeable."

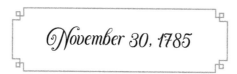

November 30, 1785

The General Court of Massachusetts passed an act for incorporating the plantation called Pearsontown in the county of Cumberland into a town by the name of Standish in honor of Myles Standish of Pilgrim fame.

The Chadbourne house at Sebago Lake Village burned. The house was erected in 1843 and was 3 1/2 stories. There was a dance hall on the third floor that was later made into rooms. Accommodations and all one could eat could be had there for $1 a day. Henry Chadbourne was the proprietor until his death in 1875. His widow ran the house until 1908, when Harry W. Roberts bought the house. He died in 1912 and his widow lived there until it burned.

Portland Press Herald, December 2, 1918

Other information seems to indicate that the house was built in 1814 by Benjamin Chadbourne and later kept by his sons William & Henry. Located on Route 35 where the Water company building is now located, this point on the shore of the lake is still known as Chadbourne's Landing. It burned from an overheated stove pipe.

THE CHADBOURNE — SEBAGO LAKE ME.
HARRY F. ROBERTS PROP.

The Standish High School Basketball team opened their season with a 108-13 victory over Casco High School the first game of their 14-1 season, losing only to Norway High School in the Lewiston small schools tournament by an end of the game long shot from the middle of the floor which decided the game. Besides the being runners-up at Lewiston, they won the Triple C Championship with two decisive wins over Cape Elizabeth and won the Gorham Normal Tournament.

Standish High School Basketball 1932
Small School Tourney Champions, 2nd Place at Lewiston, 1st Place at Gorham

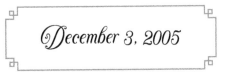

December 3, 2005

Lynn Brown, Assistant Principal at Bonny Eagle High School, was named Maine's Assistant principal year for 2005.

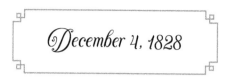

December 4, 1828

To **James Hasty Jr.** Clerk of the Town of Standish: I hereby give you notice that I did on the 29th day of November last, find in said Town, one large bar of iron, the name owner of which is unknown - **Aza Mayo**

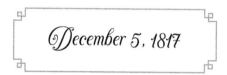

December 5, 1817

The Justices of the Circuit Court of Common Pleas granted a petition signed by **William Tompson, Jacob York** and 24 others for a straight road from Standish through Gorham to Portland. This road is the present Route 25 to Gorham. There was some discussion about making this a toll road.

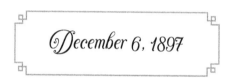

December 6, 1897

Sargent G. Emery was paid twenty dollars for chasing dogs. The dogs were killing sheep in Standish Village.

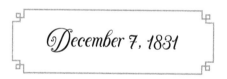

December 7, 1831

This Day record of **Samuel Phinney** four sheep for which I promise to pay him one half of the lambs and one half of the wool that is to one half of the increase for the use of them and take good care of them so long as both agree accidents or sickness happening to said sheep is Phinney's loss. **Joseph Hasty**

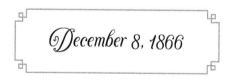

December 8, 1866

FROM THE DIARY OF JOHN P. MOULTON

Warm, commenced to rain about 3pm. I went up with Uncle Josiah on the Landing on the Jim Libby Pit and helped load a canal boat with wood. I wheel wood on board. Leander out here is the one hand and played chess. (Photo at right.)

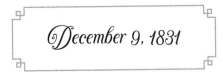
December 9, 1831

I certify that I have delivered to **Samuel Phinney** my gun & equipment and uniform coat that he may sell them at public or private sale and the money to go to an Execution which Samuel Phinney has against me. **William McCorrison**

William McCorrison was born in Buxton in 1792 and married Sally Lowell in Standish in 1819. He is not listed as a soldier of the war of 1812. Most likely he was a member of the Standish Militia.

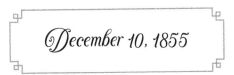
December 10, 1855

Know All Men by these Presents That I, **Francis Marean** of Standish in the Country of Cumberland in consideration of the sum of fifty dollars in hand well and truly paid before signing sealing and delivery of these presents by **Leander M. Thorn** of Said Standish in receipt thereof I do acknowledge, have granted, bargained, and sold, by these presents do grant, bargain, and sell unto the said Leander - One horse, of a dark bay color, the same I had of **Charles Tompson** and one horse of a light red or sorrel color, the same I had of Aaron Marean - The same were in my possession and use - Twenty dollars and interest in sixty days, according to the terms of a note by hand of this date given by said Francis to said Leander and if the said Francis note dated Nov. 19, 1855 payable to **Aaron Marean** or order for the sum of thirty dollars and interest in ninety days signed by said Francis and said Leander as his surety - then this bill of sale and said notes shall be void. - Received and Recorded by the Town Clerk

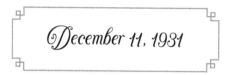

December 11, 1931

The Standish High School Basketball team demolished the Fryeburg Academy Class Champions, 76 to 22. Lombard, Lewis, and Lindquist led the team in the romp.

Roland Warren — Roy Lombard — Roland Lewis — Coach Rupert Johnson

Carl Bodge — Stanley Austin — Norman Lindquist — Willard Austin

Walter Libby — James Rand — Raymond Cleaves

Standish High School 1931 Basketball Cumberland County Champions

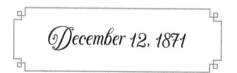

December 12, 1871

"The Sebago Lake, Maine Post Office was established with Mr. Joseph S. Webster the first Postmaster. The Post Office was situated in the corner of Mr. Webster's store which was on the lot where the present Farnum's general store is located, The old store burned about 1900."

From the Dedication of the New Sebago Lake Post Office on August 20, 1967

We know that the Post Office in the early 20th Century was housed in Rich's Store, now Walker's Landing sandwich shop. (Photo at right.)

1947

December 13, 1862

Melville H. Cooper of Company F, 17th Maine Infantry, was killed in action at Fredericksburg "The first in the Regiment to fall in battle"

On Saturday the 13th of December, the 17th Maine crossed the Rappahannock river downstream of Fredricksburg and took positions in the fields southwest of Fredricksburg replacing the retreating troops of Major General George Meade where they repelled numerous assaults from the troops of General Stonewall Jackson. It would be on the afternoon of the 13th during the rebel assaults that Melville Cooper most likely was killed. Cooper was one of two men of the 17th that died that day.

Wikipedia

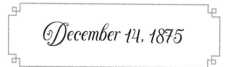

December 14, 1875

BONNY EAGLE ITEMS.—On Thursday, the 7th inst., a Mrs. Pugsley, employed as housekeeper for Samuel J. Porter, met with a very painful accident in falling down the chamber stairs, dislocating her shoulder, besides receiving other injuries.

There is one case of small pox at Bonny Eagle (Standish side of the river). We are glad to learn that every precaution is being used to prevent the spreading of the disease and that the patient is rapidly convalescing.

The Advent Quarterly Conference met at their church at Bonny Eagle on Thursday, the 8th inst. Elders Hill, Sweet, Tripp, Haines, Gay and Stevens of this state, and Samuel G. Lowe of Boston, Mass., being present. Meetings continuing through the week have been largely attended. On the Sabbath Mr. Lowe and Mark Stevens preached powerful sermons to a very full house.

Portland Daily Press - Bonny Eagle News

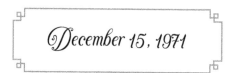

December 15, 1971

The last Lexington elm in Standish was taken down. It stood in front of the "Old Landmark", an Inn and Stables built about 1800 by **Edward Tompson** and located on the corner where Webster's Service Station now stands. It was brought from Lexington Massachusetts and planted at the end of the Revolution.

The tree was indeed an "Independence Elm" from Lexington MA, one of several to be planted in Standish at the end of the Revolutionary War. Many towns in Maine, and probably other states, planted elm trees from Lexington Massachusetts commemorating the Battle of Lexington on April 19, 1775, now called Patriots Day, the first battle of the War and the historic ride of Paul Revere and William Dawes.

The Linns will give their entertainment, the famous educated dogs, moving pictures and illustrated songs at Pythian Hall (in Steep Falls) this evening and tomorrow night. This company have given their entertainment in several nearby towns and it was very much appreciated.

Portland Evening Express

Great Falls, Gorham, To the Selectmen of Standish,

Gentlemen, I have this day been called to see a daughter of **John Gilman** who I think has Smallpox in a modified form. I know not if her husband is able to pay the bills, if not I must call on your town for payment. I give you these proper notices that you may act as your duties require in the matter.

Yours Truly, **J. Addison Parsons**

**North Gorham
looking down the hill towards the pond**

Sir, Please today Mr. **Eben Shaw** the sum of three pounds six shillings that sum being due him for bricks carried to the schoolhouse. **Isaac L. Thompson** & **George Freeman**, Selectmen. To Deacon **Jonathan Philbrick**, Treasurer of Standish (Meetinghouse district)

I do hereby certify, that I have raised during the year 1838, one hundred & ten - bushels of *"good sound and well husked ears of corn"* for which I claim the bounty provided by law therefor. I further certify, the said corn is my property, and has never received a bounty from the Treasurer of any town or plantation whatever (Signed,) **Eben R Shaw**

I do hereby certify, that I have raised during the year 1838, sixty one bushels of well cleaned wheat, for which I claim the bounty provided by law therefor. I further certify, that said wheat is my property, and has never received a bounty from the Treasurer of any town or plantation whatever (Signed,) **Eben R. Shaw**

Bounties on the growth of wheat and corn, amounting to about eight cents per bushel on wheat and four cents on corn, were paid to farmers of Maine who grew over fifty bushels.

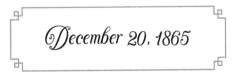

December 20, 1865

Windham, Selectmen of Standish, Gentlemen, A day or two since I sent you a note by private conveyance informing you a case of Smallpox was in progress at **John Gilman**'s in your town - above Great Falls. Fearing that might not reach you, I send you this by mail. His daughter, Mrs. Howes who resides in Boston came home on a visit two or three weeks ago and is now sick of Smallpox at her father's. I thought, when the eruption first appeared, that it might be a case of moderate severity, but now it appears genuine and may become severe. I wrote you, say now, that if her husband is not able to pay the bills I must look to your town to pay her medical bills. Mr. Gilman's family have all been exposed, but I am using every precaution to prevent them having it. I think it may be well for you to come over and arrange for them with me. I shall try and visit them in the morning and you can meet me at Great Falls - at Parker's Store.

Yours very truly, J. **Addison Parsons**

Asa Douglass Store 1915-1926

STORE POST OFFICE, NORTH GORHAM, ME, 33.

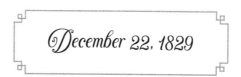

December 21, 1829

State of Maine: Cumberland s.s... To the Sheriff of our county of Cumberland, or his deputy:

We command you to attach the goods or estate of the first parish in the Town of Standish to the value of five hundred dollars and summons the said parish —(if they may be found in your precinct) to appear before our Justices of our court of Common Pleas next to be holden at Portland, within, and for our said County of Cumberland, on the third Tuesday of June AD 1833 then and there in our said court to answer unto **Daniel Marrett** of said Standish in a plea of the case for that the said Parish by their assessors **Green Cram** and **Benjamin Poland** at Standish on the twenty first day of December 1829 gave their order in writing of that date directed to **James Hasty Junior** then Treasurer there and thereby directing and

requesting their said treasurer or his successor in that office to play to the plaintiff two hundred dollars and interest thereon until the same should be paid - being the sum then due and owing from said Parish to the plaintiff and the plaintiff there afterward on the _____ day of ____ presented the said order to said Hasty then and there being the Treasurer of said Parish accepted the same - whereby said Parish became liable and in consideration thereof promised then and there to pay the plaintiff said sum on demand...

The document goes on but Rev. Daniel Marrett, the plaintiff, wants to be paid what he believes he is owed and has taken the Parish to Court for the four year old bill. This is at the time a schism developed in the church which was the heart of the dispute.

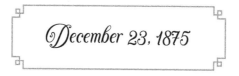

December 22, 1829

The Ecclesiastic Council meets in Standish regarding Daniel Marrett's resignation from the Unitarian Church (The Old Red Church) and Rev. Tenney's appointment. A petition was filed to protest Rev Tenney's appointment but the Council went ahead and approved Tenney.

Reverend Tenney was just too liberal for many in the parish. This led to a sizable portion of the parish to split with the Unitarians and establish (and build) the Evangelical Congregational Church nearby.

December 23, 1875

Items of Maine News.

There are four cases of small pox in Standish.

From the Maine Farmer

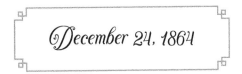

December 24, 1864

FROM THE DIARIES OF JOHN P. MOULTON

Cloudy this morning, spit snow a little, cleared off about 9. I went up to the corner after some things, came home and chored round till 1 11/2 and then went up and fixed for making hoops. In the eve at home reading the New York World. Got a letter from **Harrison P. Ward**. Pond froze over this morning.

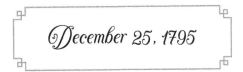

December 25, 1795

Myrick Paine brought his family to Watchic Pond and built a home, followed by three brothers. For several generations they were the only settlers on the pond. Ever since the country around has been known as the Paine Neighborhood. About 1827, **John Paine** built two pipe organs in a house near Watchic Brook, which is the outlet of the pond. Tradition says when he completed the first he had to remove the side of the house in order to get it out and take it to a nearby town for use in a Congregational Church.

He sold one to a Limington church. In 1907 there were 17 cottages and Camp Tuckernauck on the pond.

Myrick Paine Homestead

The temporary bridge over the Saco river between Standish and Limington was taken out by ice floes.

ARRESTED ON SERIOUS CHARGE

Steep Falls Man Brought Here To Face Accusation of Assault

Michael Sarara, - employed on the new dam at Steep Falls, was arrested this morning by Deputy Sheriff **Charles R. Murch** of Baldwin, on, a charge of assault with serious intent on Mrs. Odette, wife of **Napoleon Oddette**, a wood chopper, who lives in a little shack about a mile from Steep Falls. Sarara went to the shack yesterday and threw Odette out and locked the door. Mrs. Odette was in the shack with her four children. Sarara attempted to assault her but the woman's husband broke in the door before the woman was injured. Sarara, as he left the shack, was followed for some distance by Odette but as Sarara threatened him with a revolver he gave up the chase. This morning he was arrested by Deputy Murch at the store at Steep Falls and brought to this City. He was intoxicated at the time of the attempted assault.

Portland Express Advertiser

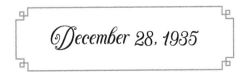

December 28, 1935

FROM THE DIARY OF GILBERT MOULTON OF SEBAGO LAKE VILLAGE

Pleasant and cold, at home all day and evening. This has been a very cold disagreeable day. The lower bay has frozen over and there is four inches of ice in it. 4 above tonight.

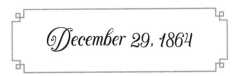

December 29, 1864

Biddeford, Gentlemen, As to the family of **Thomas Nason**, I again address you, deeming it my duty to keep you informed as to their status or situation. All their children, five in number, have been dangerously sick - two have died - one was buried yesterday and the other the week before. Beside to provision and fuel for the family I have provided them one pair sheets and one pair pillow cases, and one dress for Mrs. Nason - not before application of the neighbors to our overseers of poor was made, and from them to me, and they were provided with economy considered as to the interest of Standish. The statement that they had not a change of sheets in the house was made by those who took care of them by night, which was the cause of this provision which no doubt was true. If it would not be too much trouble I think it might be well to look to the matter yourselves - at least it would perhaps be more satisfactory to you - it is truly a hard case - Nason himself has not been able to earn anything of late - or since the children were taken sick; however I think he will now be able to earn something this week. Most respectfully yours, **Elias Harmon**.

Biddeford
Alfred Street
1870's

CHARLES HENRY SMITH EARNED THE MEDAL OF HONOR

Smith's official Medal of Honor citation reads: Rank and organization: Coxswain, U.S. Navy. Born: 1826, Maine. Accredited to: Maine. G.O. No.: 59, 22 June 1865.

On board the USS Rhode Island which was engaged in rescuing men from the stricken USS Monitor in Mobile Bay, on December 30, 1862. After the Monitor sprang a leak and went down, Smith courageously risked his life in a gallant attempt to rescue members of the crew. Although he, too, almost lost his life during the hazardous operation, he had made every effort possible to save the lives of his fellow men.

The President of the United States of America, in the name of Congress, takes pleasure in presenting the Medal of Honor to **Coxswain Charles H. Smith**, *United States Navy, for extraordinary heroism in action while serving on board the U.S.S. Rhode Island which was engaged in saving the lives of the officers and crew of the U.S.S. Monitor near Cape Hatteras, North Carolina, 30 December 1862. Participating in the hazardous rescue of the officers and crew of the sinking Monitor, Smith, after rescuing several of the men, became separated in a heavy gale with other members of the cutter that had set out from the Rhode Island, and spent many hours in the small boat at the mercy of the weather and high seas until finally picked up by a schooner 50 miles east of Cape Hatteras.*

There were two **Charles Henry Smiths** *who earned the Medal of Honor during the Civil War. The other was Major General Charles Henry Smith of the 1st Maine Cavalry who earned his medal at St. Mary's Church, Virginia on June 24, 1864. He was born in Hollis.*

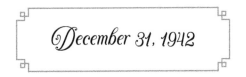

December 31, 1942

FROM THE DIARY OF GILBERT MOULTON OF SEBAGO LAKE

Clowdy with some snow in the morning but cleared off before noon, quite warm, at home all day and evening. Alice came out home tonight. They found **Roland Woodbury**'s wife's father dead in his bed this morning, he died in his sleep. **Percy Manchester** who lived up to Steep Falls committed suicide yesterday, he blew his head off with a 30-30 rifle, he and his brother lived alone on a farm and his brother was in the Hospital in Portland. 20 above tonight. Good by 1942.

Biography

Bruce Douglass is the President of the Standish Historical Society working with a group of volunteers who are passionate about the rich history of Standish Maine. He is a retired Chemistry and Earth & Space Sciences teacher, Girl's Track & Field and Girls Cross Country Coach at Ledyard High School in Ledyard, CT. He has been a genealogist for over 50 years. Growing up in Scarborough, Maine, he retired to Standish, paradise, on Sebago Lake

Although this is Bruce's first published book, he has previously compiled his grandfather's Sebago Lake camp diary, his father and grandmother's correspondence during WWII, his father-in-law's WWII letters from Leyte in the Pacific, and his mother and her mother's cookbooks.

Acknowledgments

Karen Swasey, who introduced me to **Lil Barcaski** and GWN Publishing who have produced this fabulous book.

Pam Slattery-Thomas, Glenna Jamison, Craig & Diane Herrick, Karen Herrick, Claudia White, Charles Ruby, and **Dennis O'Brien** - the stalwarts of the Standish Historical Society.

All proceeds from this book goes to the Standish Historical Society building fund.

Printed in the USA
CPSIA information can be obtained
at www.ICGtesting.com
LVHW061345230624
783775LV00004B/9